D1124522

Professors and Gods

By the same author

Professors and Gods

LAST OXFORD LECTURES ON POETRY

Roy Fuller

ST. MARTIN'S PRESS   NEW YORK

AFFILIATED PUBLISHERS: Macmillan Limited, London
— also at Bombay, Calcutta, Madras and Melbourne

Contents

Contents

Foreword
and Dedication

My book *Owls and Artificers* (1971) contained the first six lectures I gave as Professor of Poetry in the University of Oxford. The present book contains the remaining lectures of my five years' tenure of the Chair. A few passages are derived from literary journalism. The lecture on the poetry of the Thirties has one or two origins, and its penultimate form consisted of a personal anthology of Thirties poetry, with a commentary. For Oxford I decided to cut out most of the illustrative poetry and to expand the commentary. Something was thereby lost, for I had mainly gone for poems omitted by their authors from the canon of their work, or appearing there in revised versions. However, I hope enough remains of the original intent to encourage an exploration of books and periodicals actually published during the period.

A. C. Bradley dedicated his *Oxford Lectures on Poetry* 'To My Oxford Friends'. I repeat that dedication here, and would include university and college staff whose courtesy and help eased my years of office.

Acknowledgment and thanks are due to the editors of *The Times Literary Supplement*, *Tagus*, *The Michigan Quarterly Review* and *The Southern Review* where several of the lectures have already been printed.

R. F.

The Radical Skinhead

Over a decade has passed since C. P. Snow gave the Rede Lecture at Cambridge entitled *The Two Cultures and the Scientific Revolution*, a performance which in its published form drew down the wrath of F. R. Leavis in the Richmond Lecture at the same place a few years later. When Dr Leavis's lecture was published in the *Spectator* it led to a great deal of controversy, particularly in the correspondence columns of that paper, which I suppose today is mostly forgotten. But my feeling is that the subject of the controversy, though apparently flogged to death, is still of interest as well as of importance. It is a subject, like pornography or comprehensive education, that most people have views about, and views which are rarely felt to be completely expressed by the arguments of others, however apparently exhaustive. Though there were various ramifications, the essential question that divided Lord Snow and Dr Leavis was this: are there, as Snow maintained, two cultures, the literary and the scientific, which need to be brought together; or is the vital thing, as Leavis said, the prior cultural achievement — 'the creation of the human world, including language'?

It's not at all my purpose to be in the least thorough in

summarizing the views of the protagonists, and at the moment I
will only mention that Snow's position enabled him to point out
the advantages the average scientist had in being far more inward
with literary culture than the literary man with scientific culture.
Thus though the scientist was quite likely to possess and play a
record of Beethoven's Choral Symphony, the literary man was
extremely unlikely to be able to state the Second Law of
Thermodynamics. Needless to say, simple and catchy opposi-
tions of this sort got Leavis on the raw, but we may feel that the
damage he inflicted on the side had greater effect than his
asseveration of the sovereignty of human relations and human
language. In particular he refused to separate his assessment of
Snow as ex-scientist, ex-civil servant and novelist from the views
expressed in the Rede Lecture, and since that assessment was
jaundiced the controversy on Leavis's part was conducted with
blighting scorn.

However, Leavis's tough *ad hominem* treatment of Snow does
not account for the opposition his lecture aroused, though it may
have prompted some of his opponents to unmask themselves. In
the *Spectator* correspondence only two or three names of any note
ranged themselves on Leavis's side. One was his publisher, who
merely pointed out that the charge of envy was misconceived,
since Leavis's books were all in print and sold steadily in their tens
of thousands. Another was Robert Conquest, who even in those
remote days used the occasion for a salvo against the Kremlin.
The anti-Leavisites were a quite formidable bunch, ranging from
J. D. Bernal on the left to Lord Boothby on the right, and
including the poet Edith Sitwell, the painter Michael Ayrton, and
that ineffable writer of letters to the Press, G. Richards of Poole.
Many of these correspondents were rude, not in the engaged way
of Leavis himself in his lecture, but with a gratuitous insolence
that showed how excruciatingly Leavis had managed to knock
their concepts.

I was reminded of this anti-Leavis line-up not very long ago at a
literary gathering where speeches were made, and several
derogatory references to Leavis drew not only applause and

murmurs of assent but also audible remarks of a facetious cast. I speculated afresh as to why Leavis was so hated. For it is a curious thing that though, as his publisher confirmed, his books sell in continuing large quantities and his pupils and his pupils' pupils have come to occupy prominent positions in the educational and literary establishments, the opposition to Leavis is, I would guess, as vocal and nearly as numerous as ever it was. In a sense it must be felt to be more deeply entrenched than, say, thirty years ago, for the original run of *Scrutiny*, the re-print of that review, and Leavis's continuing publications have failed to reduce it. I don't myself see the reason for the opposition as being contributed to to any great extent by Leavis's own personality. No doubt he is far too touchy. There is often more than a hint of megalomania and paranoia on his side of arguments. The image of the open-necked shirted bicyclist in close touch with the springs of life is unendearing to the sessile littérateur. Leavis has plugged his literary favourites with a disc-jockey's single-mindedness, though his sympathy has been largely closed to developments in imaginative literature since his own youth. But such idiosyncrasies may be found in most artists. The Leavis opposition arises from deeper causes, arises in fact from the nature of culture in our society, which is why it is perennially renewed.

If we ask ourselves, for example, why Edith Sitwell intervened in an argument about the two cultures I think we can only reply that deep down she felt her own art to be threatened by the standards Leavis has applied to poetry, and by the line of tradition he has found in modern poetry. The opposition of Professor Bernal, a scientist sympathetic to the Communist revolution, despite the turns it has taken behind the Iron Curtain, surely came from his feeling that the Leavisite critical method might discover deficiencies even in a culture of considerable achievement, supported by society at large. I think it is this combination, in the Leavisian view, of high textual standards and a strong, however incompletely defined, sense of right social conduct that provokes from the general run of men of letters (and from some academics, too) the prejudice, often of such an irrational and

vehement kind that one is reminded of similar feelings attached
to colour or to Jewishness.

And I think that where, in the Richmond Lecture, the
susceptibilities of such people were hit was not at all in Leavis's
denial of the problem of the two cultures but in his questioning
the values of the literary culture as it is assumed to exist. Unlike
Snow (whose own conduct in the controversy, it must be
emphasized, was marked by his typical large-mindedness, very
far from prejudice of any kind) the opponents of Leavis were
mostly not in the least concerned with healing the so-called
breach between science and literature, but rather in preserving
their own places in the cultural scheme of things. Leavis's attack
on Snow's reputation as a novelist, on the culture of the 'heavy'
Sunday newspapers, his reference to the sour academic attitude
to T. S. Eliot in the Thirties — these were what exacerbated the
broad cultural masses. For in our society a process as rigorous as
any scientific law tends to make the ruling literary culture a
middlebrow culture, however much its creators and arbiters see
themselves otherwise. The mere acceptance of an Eliot, the mere
exposure of the pretensions of middlebrow writers of the past,
don't much prevent subsequent Eliots from being found in-
digestible, subsequent middlebrows from being hailed as master-
poets, master-novelists.

It may be objected that to a considerable degree Leavis is
fighting the battles of the past, that in recognizing new talent, in
making a proper hierarchy of the talent we have, we order things
much better in 1970 than they did in the 1930s. Naturally,
conditions don't stand still. Certain young critics have stiffened
up the culture of the Sunday newspapers and they wouldn't have
been likely to have had such a chance in the Thirties. And the
tendency to trendiness, the very reflections of the changes in
literary fashion, do make the papers more open than in days of
yore to the acceptance of valid experiment and dissident ideology.
But when such things have been said, don't we still find in the
Sunday papers (and the term may also signify other periodicals)
the constant wrong emphases and selections, and the kowtowing

to other than aesthetic standards, characteristic of middlebrow culture? I think there is no doubt that though class, wealth and education play a smaller part in the process than formerly, a middlebrow establishment is constantly in the process of formation, a reef to which many stray and originally independent organisms come to adhere. I keep to the word 'middlebrow' though it is unsatisfactory and imprecise. The culture of that establishment has highbrow and academic attachments. But by and large its standards and calibre fall short of the best the age can confer. Those who enter it must find, if their attainments are not tailored for it, that in some degree and in some directions they are pandering to the audience envisaged by the culture — even in such relatively small respects as being given the wrong books to review, of having withheld from them the very books whose reception their opinion might render more tepid.

I realize that it can be argued that the rather old-fashioned categories of middlebrow and highbrow have quite changed. Saul Bellow, for example, the American novelist, has said that simultaneously the writer has become a prominent social figure, while the highbrow element in art has been absorbed by television, advertising, fashion, the movies and the other media, and mashed into a meaningless porridge. Thus, though more nominal attention is paid to the writer, his real influence has been reduced. For myself, I think this view has in fact middlebrow tinges. It is true that the media today pay a great deal of attention to writers and artists, making of them characters in the endless journalistic soap opera. But they are usually writers and artists of essentially middlebrow cast: such interest is never aroused, or is quickly lost, in writers and artists of the finest calibre. The journalism of Norman Mailer is instructive in this connection. Mailer clearly expects himself to be recognized by reporters, by the police, by demonstrating crowds (though one must interpolate here the significant fact that in a poll taken during his campaign when he ran for mayor in New York sixty per cent of the persons polled had never heard of him — see the *New York Review of Books*, 24 September, 1970). In this expectation he is rarely disappointed. But he retains the middlebrow delusion that it is the quality of his creative work that has led to his recognizable eminence, and not the acceptability of that work to a second-rate audience and the making of his personality notorious by the popular media. I can't think that the way of a great creative talent has in any serious respect been made easier by the fashionable trends of our time. Indeed, it seems to me that where the trends have been taken to extremes, as in the United States, it is harder now than it was twenty or forty years ago for many serious writers and artists to get a proper showing at all.

Of course, it is the very existence of the establishment I have referred to that helps to make Snow's concept of the two cultures unreal or unmeaningful. There is not just one literary culture for the scientist to clothe himself in to make himself a whole man. Scientists in this respect are at the mercy of the men of letters who dominate the organs of literary opinion, and have no greater likelihood than other Queen's subjects of getting their tips from, say, the *Review* than from the *Sunday Times*. Those who sucked in the Second Law of Thermodynamics with their mother's milk are just as prone as the scientifically ignorant to believe in literary myths.

Leavis's invocation, therefore, of a prior cultural achievement must be of enormous appeal to those, like myself, who may be thought to be literary snobs. However much I feel myself compelled to agree with his judicious critics (and there are some) when his faults are listed (and some of them I listed earlier myself), on re-reading him I start assenting again and again out of my deepest convictions. Certainly it is not possible, without condemning oneself to Leavis's harshness, to judge the literature created by one's contemporaries by the standards of the literature that has survived from the past. On the other hand, it seems to me that the natural, in-built indulgence one must show to those creators who are grappling with the problems and phenomena of our time is enough to enable one to admit as valid and good sufficient of present-day art. No special or extraneous standards are required in this field. Stravinsky, whose literary brilliance comprised some wise as well as many silly sayings, put the point about music in a

characteristically extreme way: 'Con-temp: "with the times".
Con-temp music is the most interesting music that has ever been
written, and the present moment is the most exciting in music
history. It always has been. Nearly all con-temp music is bad, too,
and so was it ever.' But the interest and excitement to be found in
new art, if it is not to be mere King's Road (or Little Clarendon
Street) swooning over fresh fashions, must surely be accompanied
by sharp discrimination — a discrimination in fact which ought to
be even more violent than the discrimination employed in relation
to art of the past. Admirers of George Eliot may admit some virtue
in Trollope: admirers of Sylvia Plath will admit virtue in Anne
Sexton at their peril. The health, indeed, of any literary period may
be felt to depend on the amount of the discrimination it exercises.
Looking back, for example, to so recent a period as the Thirties,
one recalls that however undifferentiated it may now appear it
was in fact particularly an epoch when 'the rank of every poet was
well-known', and not only that but a time when every poet was
tabbed with a tendency, a fate. Moreover, many of the rigorous
judgements then made are being supported by time: for instance,
that Stephen Spender was wrong to turn back, as he said in his
foreword to a collection published in 1939, 'to a kind of writing
which is more personal'; that in the mid-Thirties Louis MacNeice
was writing in a style which raised him above all the then new
poets except Auden.

I don't seem to find among the young now sufficient literary
discrimination. Undoubtedly they have their favourites but this is
more akin to picking the coconut wheels from a bag of liquorice
allsorts than judging the nutriment of the whole. It's here that
Leavis ought to be of the greatest value. As a textual critic he is by
no means infallible (and on a subsequent occasion I shall glance at
this side of his work). I suppose close attention to contemporary
texts is what is most needed to sort out non-skill from skill, the
phoney from the genuine, the incoherent from the complicated,
though in the present atmosphere of literary creativity I don't see
much prospect of this being done in any influential way. But Leavis
as a moral critic is particularly persuasive and it is precisely in that

field that one might be sanguine about his influence exerting itself among young writers and readers. Some of the most telling passages in his Richmond and subsequent lectures concern the vulgarity of intention behind, the vulgarity in expression of, middlebrow culture. It is an extraordinary thing, however, that though in the lecture room and the tutorial the young may assent to a discipline that abhors the cliché, left to their own devices they may well become cliché-masters, their own creative work following the current second-rate, their editorial and journalistic work copying the papers viable in the commercial world or at best prefiguring such papers of the future. One might expect the young, for example, to eschew that most vulgar of all ways of attempting to give interest and significance to literature and art — pornography. But this is not always so. Pornography is by no means an exclusively infantile disease, but its spores, floating across the Atlantic, have found a fertile breeding ground in some young writers, even poets.

I spoke earlier of something incompletely defined at the heart of Leavis's beliefs. It is to do with that ultimate appeal to 'the human' which he so eloquently expresses, and which he often augments by invoking the fiction and criticism of D. H. Lawrence. Undoubtedly there is a sense in which we can understand Leavis in this. Lawrence was a literary artist and a human being of extraordinary sensitivity and creative facility. His response to the world of nature and his delineation of human relations is something recognizable as worthy of emulation. But his elevation in Leavis's thought to the position of final arbiter gives cause for unease. On the preliminary point of style, I think a good deal of Lawrence would be rejected by many and not merely by those who, like myself, began in adolescence with a blind love affair with the work, and, having fallen out of love, have never really been able to look at it again with the required dispasion. Then in the terms in which the problems of society have been presented in our time (and Lawrence's time) — political terms, above all — he is not a reliable guide. The movements of his thought here (when his thought dwells on the matter) are too frequently in the direction of élite authoritarian control, and this side of him is made all the more sinister by the unscientific nonsense he sometimes talked about blood and guts and race.

I don't quite know where Leavis would have been without Lawrence. It's interesting that Leavis took up the cause of literary standards just when that remarkable magazine *The Calendar of Modern Letters* was laying them down by disappearing from the scene. It wasn't merely lack of support that caused *The Calendar* to fold. Towards the end of the Twenties Edgell Rickword, and others associated with it, moved towards a position where they conceived that revolutionary politics was a more urgent and relevant activity than revolutionary literary criticism. It's worth recalling that in 1933, some time after *The Calendar* ceased publication, Leavis wrote the introduction to a volume of selections from its critical pages. There he asked himself whether *The Calendar*'s profound anxiety about a moribund literary tradition didn't condemn itself as patently futile. Shouldn't so deep a concern occupy itself instead with fundamentals? In other words, shouldn't an editor as serious as Rickword devote himself to the regeneration of society, rather than the regeneration of literature? Leavis answered these questions in the negative, as now we can anticipate he would. It gives a measure of the difficulties of a serious artist in a commercial society to contemplate the careers of Leavis and of Rickword since that time. Rickword became a Marxist and though he was behind two subsequent magazines of quite wide readership, *Left Review* and *Our Time*, he never again occupied a really influential critical place. Leavis was luckier in being in the academic world, though his frustrations and, indeed, humiliations there far from making the life a bed of roses. And we must judge him wise, all things considered, in renouncing political commitment. The alternative commitment to literary values gave him room to manœuvre, a viewpoint from which he could not only write the valuable books on the tradition of English verse and English fiction, but also integrate into the tradition the then still-misjudged poetry of Eliot and Pound.

Indeed, as early as 1932 Leavis himself anticipated with

remarkable accuracy the advantages of his politically uncommitted position. This was in a *Scrutiny* article with the apt Shakespearean title ' "Under Which King, Bezonian?" '. In this piece Leavis quotes effectively from Trotsky's *Literature and Revolution*: 'The proletariat acquires power for the purpose of doing away with class culture and to make way for human culture.' Leavis's comment is that though Trotsky 'insists that the necessary means to this consummation is to maintain continuity' and knows that 'human culture' is at present something covered by 'bourgeois culture', he does not realize 'the delicate organic growth that "human culture" is'. And so Leavis is led to his main point, which is the necessity not only for the preservation of culture but also for its development, independent of any economic, technical or social system. For Leavis sees culture in an industrial society as being no more than an empty Wellsian Utopia or American dream unless there is, here and now, 'a concerted and sustained effort to perpetuate it, in spite of the economic process, the triumphs of engineering and the Conquest of Happiness, as something with its own momentum and life, more and more autonomous and self-subsistent'.

This, in the early Thirties, seemed to the Left a needlessly frail and impractical programme. To many, at this present time, it may seem a counsel of despair, the condemnation of culture to the scattered monasteries of a dark age. And I am aware of, and to a great degree sympathize with, the view of Leavis taken by Perry Anderson of the New Left, that his arguments are circular and idealistic (see *New Left Review*, No. 50, July–August 1968). But it has to be noted that nearly forty years have gone by during which Leavis has, despite all I've said, enlarged his influence and the application of his principles, while many with more fundamental or doctrinaire notions have tergiversated or given up the ghost or found themselves in utter isolation. Even by 1940, in another *Scrutiny* article called 'Retrospect of a Decade', Leavis was able to say, with justification, that the importance of the function *Scrutiny* modestly existed to serve was generally granted, that the history of the decade justified the intentions with which it was started, a vital part of those intentions being 'to stand for the human tradition as something to be fostered apart from any particular religious creed' — Leavis, of course, including Marxism in that term. Leavis's successes against the political history of his times has for me one overwhelmingly important lesson, and that is that the Left cannot be any less scrupulous than he has been about the transmission of culture, about truth in our everyday affairs, and about the absence of cruelty in our faith.

Another three decades on, I think we must say that, though Leavis's 1940 defence of his position still stands up, the price paid can be seen to be great. If *Scrutiny*'s service to culture was, in Leavis's term, necessarily modest, *Scrutiny* itself has now gone and the service in its pristine form is carried on by one (or, rather, two) pairs of hands. I've noted the curious gap between the measure of academic acceptance, of student acceptance, of Leavis's literary standards, and the general literary culture, Sunday papers culture, scarcely improved since the days of the Thirties — to say nothing of the dismal mass of work being turned out by young writers. But there is also another sphere in which the effect of Leavis's efforts may be thought to have proved disappointing, and that is the university and the desired primacy there of the English School.

The supreme importance, for Leavis, of the university follows from his rejection of political instrumentation, for where else could he have found disinterested standards, uncommercial motives, an arena of possible influence on the country's best minds, both budding and mature? And his appeal for moral sanction to the human, his sense of language as the paramount mark of the human, similarly centres his concept of the English university in English studies. Leavis's appeal here I, for one, find noble and moving, as would anyone not entirely heartless who had spent a large part of his life grappling with language and is now by a freak of the ballot privileged to add to a university's tradition, even if merely an unworthy name. The appeal is romantic in the best sense. Its elevation of creativity and humanity and language, and its relating of those things to science reminds us irresistibly of

Shelley's essay *A Defence of Poetry*. Poetry, Shelley said, is 'that to which all science must be referred', and: 'The cultivation of those sciences which have enlarged the limits of the empire of man over the external world, has, for want of the poetical faculty, proportionally circumscribed those of the internal world; and man, having enslaved the elements, remains himself a slave'; and again: 'We want the creative faculty to imagine that which we know; we want the generous impulse to act that which we imagine, we want the poetry of life: our calculations have outrun conception; we have eaten more than we can digest.'

But of course, behind Shelley's appealing eloquence is the political thought of William Godwin, perfectly apt for the early part of the nineteenth century in England, still stirred by the bourgeois revolution in France. The ensuing 150 years witnessed the rise of the industrial working-class, the development of the scientific socialism appropriate to its aspirations, the rise of political parties designed to bring it to power. They witnessed the deviations and failures of those parties and the terrible tyrannies designed to counter them when a chance of their prevailing seemed imminent. It is this interim which we may feel Leavis's appeal doesn't fully take account of. But it is not merely the vital mechanics of restoring to humanity the chance to be truly human that his thought omits: his educated élite are thrown into a world of commercial communications of a vulgarity Shelley never knew and which even Matthew Arnold couldn't foresee. It must seem to us that however close the university approaches Leavis's ideal, the world which lies in wait outside will remain infinitely more powerful, so that the creation of his wished-for prevailing climate of educated opinion is indefinitely postponed. Moreover, he seems to assume too readily that the university can stay in a sense outside society. But academic citadels not only are forced to surrender to fascist régimes: in rather more subtle ways they may be made to serve alien purposes. We may not have reached in this country the subservience of parts of the university to military and commercial ambitions so notorious in the United States, but who can doubt that the alienation from the university felt by some of its junior (and senior) members arises from the sense that if the crunch came the university might bow to governmental and corporate dictates?

Nevertheless, my own conviction is (and I've expressed it on previous occasions in rather different ways) that scepticism about purity of motives, insight into society's real processes, is no excuse for anarchy or barbarism. Leavis rightly rejects the mere 'jam' of technological progress, the sickly-sweet spread of affluence. Without a moral basis the gadgets of existence are meaningless. Even where technological progress is going to raise masses of people above starvation level we must look with dismay at the civil wars and political corruption that we export with our capital and our machines, as in Africa. All the more vital to preserve, through the possible, the necessary changes in our society, the standards of feeling, of language, we have learnt from the past. We are more sophisticated than Shelley, we exist in an altogether more inimical world, but the notions he inherited from Godwin are not entirely superannuated. Some words from H. N. Brailsford's *Shelley, Godwin and their Circle* occur to me; an elderly little book but I think still irreplacable. He said:

> It is a truth that outworn institutions fetter and dwarf the mind of man. It is also a truth that institutions have moulded and formed that mind. To condemn the past is in the same breath to blast the future. The true basis for that piety towards our venerable inheritance which Burke preached, is that it has made for us the possibility of advance.

Besides, how meaningless and ineffectual a literature of revolt which falls short of the standards of the past. One's almost tempted to assert that no state need fear the second-rate in art. It's significant that much of the best literature produced in the Soviet Union has coincided with that suspected or suppressed by the authorities. *Per contra*, by no means does outrageousness of style or content in art denote a revolt in favour of human values, human progress, human freedom. One has only to think of the links between Italian futurism and fascism, and in our day the hippie art that helps to lead some American youth into realms of deranged and mindless action. Indeed, in this country we have the not altogether comic phenomenon of State help being given to the creators and entrepreneurs of incoherent art, as though the encouragement of untrained actors and painters, of pornography, were an insurance against adventurous minds latching on to the analysis of reality and expressing themselves in true political terms. When the Arts Council gave a committee £15,000 to develop 'new activities in the arts' it was proposed to be spent on 'EVENTS of "new activities" ' in certain regions of England. 'Each region', the committee's proposals went on, 'will be self-governing — you can take over a village, hire an aerodrome, use the streets, or find extensive city premises: the whole EVENT could take place in a train which tours the region. You can hire a football pitch, hire uniforms and do a Peaceful Tattoo. You can publish poems on the streets. You can make music, or put an end to music. You can make theatre, or put an end to theatre.'

It would be easy to go on documenting the grotesque and sinister rebellion that conceives the alternative to an imperfect art to be non-art, to an imperfect university a non-university. Forty years ago such nihilism would have been labelled 'fascist'. And, indeed, under the fascist régimes nihilism flourished in the realm of science, too. When culture is under fire its indivisible nature is apparent, and its separation into the literary and the scientific no more than a matter of mere terminology. We cannot take for granted the patience and truth of science in its investigation of reality any more than we can take for granted similar qualities in artists dealing with the material of their art. Both activities depend on the vital prior human organization. Nature, Wordsworth said, is 'the Original of human art'. He might have said, equally, that it was the Original of human science. The delineation of nature, in both art and science, is no straightforward, automatically progressive activity: it has to be conducted against the pressures of prejudice, shibboleths, self-interest, ossified thought and social organization, all the non-human (in Leavis's term), merely material motives of man.

I know that many people find a thick streak of self-parody in Leavis, and it annoys them or makes them grin. His harping on the importance of the university and the primacy there of the English School is such a case. However, his life and experiences in the university surely make his burden understandable. Like myself, the majority of my audience is part of a university only by way of temporary tenure. But don't we who are even thus associated with the English School feel fundamentally, or at any rate initially, the obligations and opportunities that Leavis has delineated? Many of us aspire actually to add to the corpus of work to be studied and discussed by the English School; more, to continue that study and discussion here and in other places of education. On those particularly the Leavisian responsibilities lie.

I don't myself see anything priggish in trying to assume those responsibilities. Still less do I see them as beyond the powers of those who arrive here Michaelmas by Michaelmas. My two years in Oxford have confirmed what I previously conceived, that the best minds of the rising generation are not only not inferior to those of past generations but also possess special qualities of seriousness, gentleness and compassion, no doubt stemming particularly from the post-War reduction in educational exclusiveness and from better teaching and, above all, from the sense of appalling danger and unrivalled opportunity rising from the contemporary situation of humankind. Teaching (I use the convenient term though it is properly not liked by Leavis) I can't speak personally about, but I do know something of the burden of creativity. As Shelley in his essay truly said: 'The mind in creation is as a fading coal, which some invisible influence, like an inconstant wind, awakens to transitory brightness.' My experience has been with a coal full of slag, perhaps from a near-exhausted pit, but I think even brighter creative minds always see before them the peculiar dauntingness of the struggle to find fresh truth in nature expressed in language free from cliché. It's a struggle that time to some extent rewards but which no achievement can alleviate. The effort of teaching I'm sure has many parallels.

The standards exacted by true creativity, by true teaching, could

be met by many, possibly most, of the recruits to our English
School. Those standards could be carried also to the other places
and activities to which fate will consign the graduate in English.
Don't we, putting it like that, immediately begin to see the reason
for Leavis's excitement about his notion? But let's be cruelly
realistic. Let's give the fullest weight to the ossified minds and the
fashionable temptations that the new recruit will meet here, the
pressures of carelessness and corruption that lie outside. Even so,
isn't there, in the possibility of merely a comparatively few holding
on to standards, discovering and perhaps continuing 'the great
tradition' of English literature, isn't there in this a ground for hope?
It's a hope not for the transfiguration of society for, as I've said,
unlike Leavis I see the prior terms for that as political. But it is a
hope for an improvement in the quality of our literature, institu-
tions, life; above all (and here I absolutely go along with Leavis) in
the quality of the contribution this country can make to world
society, a contribution of rather more substance than armaments.
To take merely one instance: it's only through authoritativeness
here that the English-speaking world can be saved from those
American variations on the language so apt to express sentimentality, political duplicity and false values — political gobbledegook,
poetical windbaggery.

Besides, we owe to scientists the obligation to make our
discipline not less great nor less arduous than theirs. It's not that
the scientist in his hours of ease shall have a contemporary literary
culture to enjoy equal to that of the past, any more than that we
on our side best show our respect for science by being able to
recite the Second Law of Thermodynamics. The problems science
proposes to itself, the applications science makes, the very moral
fibre of scientific practitioners, arise out of that culture evolved
through the faculty that differentiates humans from the rest of
animal creation, language. A sickly language and literature mean
a sickly society, against which science itself is powerless.

Of course, one must ask oneself these days (or more likely these
nights, waking in the dead middle of them) whether one hasn't
to be even more realistic; whether the rot hasn't penetrated too

deep for there to be hope of any sort of general revival of standards in our society, as it exists and may develop in the near future. In music, for example, the degeneration of former classical tradition and the over-estimation of kitsch have reached points quite past the temporarily fashionable. It's in such acceptance of dissent on its own terms by those responsible for maintaining standards that perhaps the greatest dangers lie. The questions in this area are undoubtedly confusing, sharpened as they are by the personal positions in the arts and the universities occupied by those involved. A notice in the *New York Review of Books* not very long ago (12 February, 1970) conveniently embraced some of the issues. The subject of the notice was two books by mature American radicals, Sidney Hook and Daniel J. Boorstin, which in different ways condemned the New Left in the United States. I'm necessarily simplifying, but I think both authors, particularly Professor Boorstin, would see in the movements for student power and black power not radicalism but barbarianism, marked, as barbarianism has always been in our time, by a confused political ideology or by an absence of it, and accompanied by book-burning, pointless destruction of property, vague and un-negotiable demands. The reviewer, himself an academic, Professor of Philosophy and History of Ideas at an American University, was greatly shocked at these accusations that the new radicals had abandoned the search for meaning, lacked coherent ideas and concern for society; and in particular denied that in our society there was validity in the idea of the university being able to enjoy academic freedom — a freedom which might indeed need protection against barbarianism though the barbarians had in view a greater freedom in the end.

One can sympathize with both sides of the fence. However ludicrous or nauseating the manner of protest and the character of the protestants, how can one divorce one's sympathies where the object of the protest is one's own — the iniquity of the American part in the Vietnam war, for example? And yet how impossible to assent to the vague and dubious programmes of learning and creativity proposed by certain student demonstrators to replace certain ordered academic disciplines. Again, though it isn't necessarily easy for a senior member of a university to throw in his lot with dissenting junior members, it's the harder course, it seems to me, for the senior member to diagnose and attack the ills while maintaining culture's health. This latter position, the position it may be called of the radical skinhead, easily collects misunderstanding and undesirable allies. Say a word, for instance, against abstract art and fan letters come from those not who see abstract art's bankruptcy now but who opposed it in the year when Kandinsky saw a picture on its side and decided that 'the depiction of objects needed no place in [his] paintings and was indeed harmful to them', to wit, 1908. That is why I have thought it important to try to define an establishment in opposition to such as Dr Leavis, an opposition which is a real target for those who rightly want change and renewal in literary creation and evaluation.

Those of us engaged in the arts who have always, in Thomas Mann's famous phrase, seen the age as presenting man's destiny in political terms, have not only found it congenitally difficult to maintain a working relation with political action but have also lacked the theoretical acumen and knowledge to disentangle the political confusions of the time, especially the disastrous fragmentations of the Left. Perhaps it is a lingering illusion, but one has more and more clung on to the principles of artistic order, craftsmanship and honesty as a guide-line in social as well as interior life. These are not just bourgeois virtues. And the other simple and enduring lesson of living one's formative years in the Thirties is that anything bearing the hallmarks of fascism must be regarded with suspicion and loathing. Violence which is not provoked by the violence of the establishment; hatred of culture; despisal of history and the historical view — such things, as we have learnt through horrifying experience, are evidence not of revolution but of reaction.

Perry Anderson ended the article I've already referred to, which contained his critique of Leavis, with these words: 'a revolutionary practice within culture is possible and necessary today.

The student struggle is its initial form.' My point is that if standards are not kept during the course of revolutionary practice the chances of the standards being there when the practice has been successful are nil. The meanness, oppression and bureaucracy of a post-bourgeois culture which has lost standards will make the back-slapping, trendiness and triviality of our present Sunday newspaper culture seem like a lost Golden Age.

II

The Osmotic Sap

What once seemed to be one of Dr Leavis's most telling criticisms
of Shelley concerned the following familiar passage from the
'Ode to the West Wind':

> *Thou on whose stream, mid the steep sky's commotion,*
> *Loose clouds like earth's decaying leaves are shed,*
> *Shook from the tangled boughs of Heaven and Ocean,*
>
> *Angels of rain and lightening: there are spread*
> *On the blue surface of thine aëry surge,*
> *Like the bright hair uplifted from the head*
>
> *Of some fierce Maenad, even from the dim verge*
> *Of the horizon to the zenith's height,*
> *The locks of the approaching storm.*

Perhaps I may read Dr Leavis's paragraph of commentary,
from his chapter on Shelley in *Revaluation*:

The sweeping movement of the verse, with the accompanying
plangency, is so potent that, as many can testify, it is possible
to have been for years familiar with the Ode — to know it by

heart — without asking the obvious questions. In what respects are the 'loose clouds' like 'decaying leaves'? The correspondence is certainly not in shape, colour, or way of moving. It is only the vague general sense of windy tumult that associates the clouds and the leaves; and, accordingly, the appropriateness of the metaphor 'stream' in the first line is not that it suggests a surface on which, like leaves, the clouds might be 'shed', but that it contributes to the general 'streaming' effect in which the inappropriateness of 'shed' passes unnoticed. What again, are those 'tangled boughs of Heaven and Ocean'? They stand for nothing that Shelley could have pointed to in the scene before him; the 'boughs', it is plain, have grown out of the 'leaves' in the previous line, and we are not to ask what the tree is. Nor are we to scrutinize closely the 'stream' metaphor as developed: that 'blue surface' must be the concave of the sky, an oddly smooth surface for a 'surge' — if we consider a moment. But in this poetic surge, while we let ourselves be swept along, there is no considering, the image doesn't challenge any inconvenient degree of realization, and the oddness is lost. Then again, in what ways does the approach of a storm ('loose clouds like earth's decaying leaves', 'like ghosts from an enchanter fleeing') suggest streaming hair? The appropriateness of the Maenad, clearly, lies in the pervasive suggestion of frenzied onset, and we are not to ask whether her bright hair is to be seen as streaming out in front of her (as, there is no need to assure ourselves, it might be doing if she were running before a still swifter gale: in the kind of reading that got so far as proposing to itself this particular reassurance no general satisfaction could be extracted from Shelley's imagery).

My feeling is that this paragraph, as a link in Dr Leavis's argument against Shelley (which I'll come to in a moment), won general acceptance and has coloured the view of Shelley ever since 1936, when *Revaluation* was first published. In my own case I was always slightly uneasy that Dr Leavis seemed to be neglecting the point that Shelley's three stanzas are, after all, descriptive of a certain kind of sky; but it was not until 1960, when Desmond King-Hele published his book *Shelley: His Thought and Work*, that the rights of the matter were established.* Here is Mr King-Hele's relevant paragraph:

As Shelley sees it, about two-thirds of the sky is blue and about one-third, from nearly overhead to as far as the eye can see in the west, is covered by a high filmy layer of white, streaky mare's-tail or plume cirrus, which, as its name implies, looks like dozens of horses' tails or plumed helmets streaming in the wind. Low in the west are jagged detached clouds, scud or fractostratus, grey and watery, approaching fast in the rising wind. It is a familiar scene on the south coast of England, warning of a watery end to a fine summer's day. In the first $3\frac{2}{3}$ lines of Shelley's stanza, the *loose clouds, shed* like *earth's decaying leaves* into the airstream, are the fractostratus clouds, harbingers of rain. The *tangled boughs* from which these leaf-like clouds are shaken are those regions of air whose slightly adverse pressures, temperature and humidities make them the destined birthplace for clouds. These parcels of air, turbulent, ever-changing in shape like wind-blown boughs, contain a mixture of water vapour from *Ocean* and air from *Heaven*. The remaining five lines describe the mare's-tail cirrus, the *bright hair* spread as if on the *blue surface* of the sky, and streaming like the hair of a girl running into a strong wind. The cirrus stretches from the *horizon,* which is *dim* because obscured by the scud, to the *zenith.* The simile of the Maenads probably appears because Shelley had recently seen Maenad figures in the Uffizi Gallery at Florence: the simile is apt, for Maenads had the odd habit of rushing around with hair streaming. Since the word 'cirrus', coined by Shelley's contemporary Luke Howard, means 'a lock of hair', the emphasis on hair is justified. And, as spreading cirrus often heralds a depression, Shelley neatly links his imagery with the weather outlook in the final *locks of the*

---

* A premature judgement — see F. H. Ludlam, 'The Meteorology of Shelley's Ode', *TLS*, September 1, 1972, and subsequent correspondence in the issues of September 22 and 29. However, Professor Ludlam emphasizes Shelley's scientific accuracy.

approaching storm, a phrase which is used as a caption to a photograph of plume cirrus in Grant's *Cloud and Weather Atlas*.

Mr King-Hele adds that his explanation of the lines has been so detailed precisely because Dr Leavis 'failed to distinguish between the fractostratus and cirrus clouds'.

It's piquant that Mr King-Hele should have graduated from Cambridge with a first in Mathematics (he is now Senior Principal Scientific Officer in the Space Department at the Royal Aircraft Establishment, Farnborough). Dr Leavis's insistence on the unity of culture could scarcely have had more dramatic support. My own purpose in juxtaposing these two critical quotations (which I fear may have been all too familiar to many) has been to emphasize the common ground between the literary critic and the scientist, and, indeed, between the scientist and the poet himself. For of course, the fundamental objection which Dr Leavis is making to Shelley is his untruth to nature; and when Mr King-Hele demonstrates that in the passage from the West Wind Ode there is truth after all, the passage's prestige is restored.

Dr Leavis, in his Shelley chapter, goes on to anatomize the poetry's main deficiency — 'in . . . a general tendency of the images to forget the status of the metaphor or simile that introduced them and to assume an autonomy and a right to propagate, so that we lose in confused generations and perspectives the perception or thought that was the ostensible *raison d'être* of imagery, we have a recognized essential trait of Shelley's: his weak grasp upon the actual.' Despite the disappearance of the crutch for the argument, the passage from the West Wind Ode, the justice of this must be admitted. Mr King-Hele's book is right to emphasize Shelley's scientific interests and excellent in its disinterment of those interests in the poetry. And perhaps one more example may be given of the danger of overlooking the scientific cast of Shelley's mind:

When the lamp is shattered
The light in the dust lies dead —

When the cloud is scattered
The rainbow's glory is shed . . .

'Shed': only, says Dr Leavis, 'in the vaguest and slackest state of mind — of imagination and thought — could one so describe the fading of a rainbow.' Mr King-Hele's riposte is: 'Yet the bow is created by the internal reflexion of sunlight in waterdrops shed by the cloud, so that its glory is literally *shed* with the last drops of the shower.' Nevertheless, generally speaking, Shelley's power of employing reality in his verse is uncertain, as his use of scientific notions is faint and damaged by the peculiarities of his vocabulary and narrative style. We must feel that had his knowledge and practice of the discipline been more profound or systematic his poetry would have been greatly improved. All too often his involvement was on the level of the celebrated occasion, when Hogg visited Shelley's chaotic rooms in University College and was asked to turn the handle of an electric generating machine, the poet then attaching himself to it until his long hair stood on end.

For the nineteenth century (and after) Shelley, even more than Keats, became the prototype of the poetic character. This dubious position was achieved for him by his scientific interests being over-looked and by his dissident political opinions being taken over by working-class intellectuals, leaving for minor poets and poetry circles what A. C. Bradley characterized as his 'quivering intensity'. I think it was rarely seen how different was his fundamental brand of mind from that of Keats. Keats has a strong grasp upon the actual, but there is a provincialism in his outlook (as exhibited in his verse, at any rate) that insulates the actual from the current of thought and history in his time, resulting in a notion of beauty as a poetic objective that crippled subsequent poets with less talent for communicating sensuous experience. This weakness in Keats is symbolized for me in the despisal of science exhibited by his tire-some notion that the scientific age had robbed the rainbow of its mystery, and the weakness is, of course, even more damaging to post-Keatsian verse. 'How just, how beauteous the refractive law,' said James Thomson, contemplating the rainbow in the eighteenth century. Such a sentiment is just what is lacked by the nineteenth century — and after. In the dilute emotions of Coleridge's early verse what a relief to come on this:

On a given finite line
Which must in no way incline;
    To describe an equi-
    -lateral Tri-
    -A,N,G,L,E.
        Now let A. B.
        Be the given line
    Which must no way incline;
    The great Mathematician
    Makes this Requisition,
        That we describe an Equi-
        -lateral Tri-
        -angle on it;
Aid us, Reason — aid us, Wit!

Of course, the earlier Wordsworth, in this as in much else, had the rights of the matter. One thinks at once of the famous passage in the preface to the second edition of Lyrical Ballads, where he speaks of the poet being 'ready to follow the steps of the man of science', not only in 'any material revolution' that science may make to man's condition, but also 'carrying sensation into the midst of the objects of the science itself. The remotest discoveries of the chemist, the botanist or mineralogist will be . . . proper objects of the poet's art.' But the alienating processes of the nineteenth century tended not only to divorce the poet from the scientist but also the poet from the reality that science was making even more real. By the time of The Excursion, Wordsworth was speaking of science's 'dull eye, dull and inanimate' as being 'chained to its object in brute slavery', and forgetting the supreme importance of nature's relationship with man. It must have been annoying for scientists to read in Book IV of the poem that it was not enough for them 'with patient interest to watch / The processes of things, and

2

serve the cause of order and distinctness'. This wish for science to
be something other than it is poisons the poet's relations with it.
Part of the power of one of the greatest of nineteenth century
poems, *In Memoriam*, is its reaction to the great geological and
biological discoveries of the mid-century:

> Contemplate all this work of time,
>   The giant labouring in his youth;
>   Nor dream of human love and truth,
> As dying nature's earth and lime;
>
> But trust that those we call the dead
>   Are breathers of an ampler day
>   For ever nobler ends. They say,
> The solid earth whereon we tread
>
> In tracts of fluent heat began,
>   And grew to seeming-random forms,
>   The seeming prey of cyclic storms,
> Till at the last arose the man;
>
> Who throve and branched from clime to clime,
>   The herald of a higher race
>   And of himself in higher place,
> If he so type this work of time
>
> Within himself, from more to more;
>   Or, crowned with attributes of woe
>   Like glories, move his course, and show
> That life is not as idle ore,
>
> But iron dug from central gloom,
>   And heated hot with burning fears
>   And dipt in baths of hissing tears,
> And battered with the shocks of doom
>
> To shape and use. Arise and fly
>   The reeling Faun, the sensual feast;
>   Move upward, working out the beast,
> And let the ape and tiger die.

The use made here by Tennyson of scientific research and speculation has touches of the naïve, and there is still the impotent grasping after the notion that science misses an important part of the truth. But Tennyson's response, though shocked, is the response of the whole poetic personality, and that kind of response gets rarer, it seems to me, as the nineteenth century develops and then turns over into the poeticism of the earlier part of this century. *In Memoriam* is a poem written out of the weakness of the poet's ideological position, but since taking the weakness into account it in a way transcends it. The parallel that occurs is the poetry written by some bourgeois poets of the nineteen-thirties in the face of the overwhelming logic of Marxism.

I'm very conscious of my own naïvety in the view I'm putting forward. Still, I don't want to be taken to be saying that the recipe for poetic success is for poets to cast about in some scientific stream. Otherwise it would be wondered why Alfred Noyes's *The Torch-bearers*, for instance, a scientific epic in its way, wasn't a great poem. My point is, I suppose, that a blind or neutral attitude to science tends to insulate the poet from the spirit of his age and narrows his apprehension of reality, leading in turn to such poetically-destructive traits as sentimentalism. I've said on another occasion how sinister it seems to me, for example, that Blake's anti-scientific obscurantism has been taken up by poets whose verse is (*ipso facto*, one might say) often formless and mawkish.

Moreover, it is only a short step from Shelley's cirrus and fractostratus clouds to feel (I think with the right instinct) that there is something almost intrinsically poetic in the scientific. No doubt part of this comes from the precision of a scientific vocabulary. When readers found in the *Oxford Poetry* of 1927:

> *though we*
> *Have ligatured the ends of a farewell,*
> *Sporadic heartburn show in evidence*
> *Of love uneconomically slain* . . .

I think they must have been reassured that one undergraduate poet at least was on the right lines — though the mixing of metaphors from the surgeons' and physicians' sides of medicine would perhaps not have been admitted by the more mature Auden. Part of the tone and the achievement of the characteristic verse of the nineteen-thirties comes from this sympathy with the aims and terminology of science. Auden had a scientific family background; William Empson and Charles Madge had serious scientific interests; so, too, had Michael Roberts, one of the early entre-preneurs of the Thirties movement; Christopher Caudwell was an aeronautical correspondent and invented a differential gear; through Bronowski the poetry had links with the contemporary scientific world. Also, the way to greater realism and scope in Thirties poetry had been cleared by the anti-Georgian side of the Twenties. Part of the new tone in a poet like Edgell Rickword comes from his interest in psychoanalysis and anthropology; and one would miss the full flavour of a couplet like the following if one hadn't in mind the then current discussions about the essentially random nature of the motion of particles:

Dawn is a miracle each night debates,
Which faith may prophesy but luck dictates.

Moreover, the beliefs behind so much Thirties verse took it for granted that science was a beneficial force. To be a socialist was — is — to believe that science if not an actual is a potential good and a necessary instrument in removing social injustice.

The scientific as the intrinsically poetic. Of course, this is an idea subject to severe qualification. There was a notorious line in the Thirties written by a poet I've already referred to, Michael Roberts. The line was: 'Osmotic climbs delightful sap.' One sees that the tendency of liquids to pass through porous septa and so ascend the trunks of trees is a fact of poetic possibilities, but the line fails really to exploit those possibilities, and the epithet chosen for sap — delightful — is merely fitting out Georgianism with another pair of trousers. Roberts is rather more successful else-where, and lines like 'Down to the last abstraction Earth / Fulfils

her geodesic curve' possibly enabled later poets to pull the thing off
better. For Roberts, born in 1902, is essentially a Twenties poet:
the images from science or urban life are brought in but the poetic
aim is really not very different from that of the 'traditional' verse
of the earlier part of the century. The verse, for example, of Aldous
Huxley, beneath the rather self-consciously worn modern properties, has the old notion of being 'poetic'. Roberts's scientific
training was much more effective in his later role as anthologist
and propagandist for the new movement. C. P. Snow once
remarked that he thought the Angry Young Men movement arose
from the frustration felt by the arts chap confronted by a scientific
world, and certainly when one compares the rebellion of the
Thirties with that of the Fifties (I say nothing of the Sixties) it's
not only the political differences that are striking but also the
earlier period's scientific temper in contrast with the later's almost
total lack of interest in science, not to say anti-scientific basis. Of
course, in the last analysis the science depends on the politics, but
all the same the anthologies *New Signatures* and *New Country*
would have been quite different articles had Roberts not felt that
science and poetry were allied in the struggle against capitalist
breakdown, minority art, the decline of England. So, too, one
senses the scientific training behind the scheme of another
anthology of Roberts, *The Faber Book of Modern Verse*—the
rigorous selection of trends, the making available of American
samples, the generous representation of each poet. I'm speaking
of course, of the original edition: nothing illustrates so sharply the
sad decline of scientific and critical temper as the later editorial
tinkerings by other hands.

One's been led oneself into the osmotic sap fallacy, or something akin to it. In a book brought out to mark the centenary of
The Origin of Species I came across the remark—obvious enough
when stated, but when stated quite startling, as it seemed to me—
that mating communities are constituted by the entire species. In
most species propinquity is the overwhelming factor in the
business of mating choice, but man's mobility through artificial
modes of travel has in his case reduced the importance of that

factor. Moreover, so far as the human species is concerned, certain ideological barriers have been raised by pigmentation, though biologically, of course, the black, red, white and yellow races together constitute the mating community. In the same, or a similar, book I also read that cattle breeders, breeding for meat, breed short-legged animals, but that that design is no use for milk-producers where a large udder has got to be accommodated. The contrast here with the production of suitable human beings was notable, particularly having regard to the wide practical as well as theoretical human mating community. There seemed to be a poem in the union of these two ideas, tarted up with a reference to the human erotic taste, in mythical times at any rate, for species other than its own.

> *Mating communities are the entire*
> *Species: thus no one is too black or too*
> *Remote to fall in love with, though the briar-*
> *Cheeked, straw-haired, next-door girl will do.*

> *The thrift that got the mule, the fantasy*
> *The tiglon, cannot be applied to man*
> *Though he will always covetously eye*
> *The bull, the laurel and the swan.*

> *For meat are bred short-leggèd beasts, while milk*
> *Producers must have long to accommodate*
> *Huge udders; but the apt in our own ilk*
> *Is left to inefficient fate.*

One realizes clearly what has gone wrong here. The result is akin to those versifications of Marxist points that were written in the Thirties—that one wrote oneself—and which I think only John Cornford, under the pressure of being in the fighting in the Spanish Civil War, brought off in one or two poems. There is even the same kind of strangulated neatness that I recall only too well. And even as I was preparing this lecture I came across the poetically tempting remark, in a book by Professor David Pilbeam, *The Evolution of Man*, that it was the freeing of the human female from the straitjacket of oestrus, which limited the sex life of her ancestresses to a few hours each month, that made monogamy acceptable to the male—and hence the development of family life. That temptation has been resisted.

Oddly enough (or, rather, not oddly at all) the process of scientific discovery itself gives the clue to the working-out that alone could result in such scientific facts, and the aperçus leading from them becoming an organic part of a poem. Every poet who has read James D. Watson's brilliant book, *The Double Helix*, must have been struck by the parallels between the discovery of the structure of the DNA molecule and the composition of a poem. The most remarkable of these, I think, is the way Watson, when completely stuck with the main problem, took up a different line of research—on the tobacco mosaic virus, TMV. Though a vital component of TMV is nucleic acid, it is not DNA but another form, RNA—ribonucleic acid. A brief summary does ill justice to Watson's fascinating chapter on this, but putting the point crudely, Watson's confirmation of the helical structure of TMV was a reassurance and a spur in his subsequent return to the problems of proving and modelling the helical structure of DNA. The disparate aperçus blended, as perhaps not fully consciously Watson had prefigured. The process was, as a matter of fact, described by Freud in *The Interpretation of Dreams* with his characteristic literary precision: 'When in the course of a piece of scientific work we come upon a problem which is difficult to solve, it is often a good plan to take up a second problem along with the original one—just as it is easier to crack two nuts together than each separately.' So, occasionally, two quite separate strands of poetic thought and drafting may, if one is lucky, combine: the lesser reinforcing the main strand often in the most practical way and providing a concreteness the main strand may have lacked. My mating communities and huge udders really belong to another, alas unwritten, poem.

As I've said, the scientific temper to be seen in some of the new literature of the Twenties was vital in determining the character and direction of that of the Thirties. But if one looks now at a critical work of the Twenties with that cast—I. A. Richards's *Science and Poetry*—I think one must be surprised at the modesty of its claims. At least, I am surprised, having started writing— using that term in any serious sense—just when the Thirties began. Richards's book, scarcely more than an essay, was one in a series called 'Psyche Miniatures', part medical, part more general, published in connection with a journal of psychology called *Psyche*. It is a book that, like *Hamlet*, is full of quotations— pronouncements by Richards, in full cry as critic, that have become part of the contemporary literary consciousness. But taken as a whole it seems to me a contradictory and unsatisfactory work. I suppose its aim was to assign a role to poetry in an age already become, and likely to remain, thoroughly secular. It has as its epigraph Matthew Arnold's famous words:

> The future of poetry is immense, because in poetry, where it is worthy of its high destinies, our race, as time goes on, will find an ever surer and surer stay. There is not a creed which is not shaken, not an accredited dogma which is not shown to be questionable, not a received tradition which does not threaten to dissolve. Our religion has materialised itself in the fact, in the supposed fact; it has attached its emotion to the fact, and now the fact is failing it. But for poetry the idea is everything.

Richards wants to justify poetry's continuing importance in terms less idealistic than Arnold's, against a background less religious, more thoroughly scientific (or, at least, technological), and with a view of the human mind made more sophisticated by the discoveries of psychoanalysis. At the end of the book he seems to be envisaging, recommending, a poetry 'independent of all beliefs', and founded instead on 'the world-picture of science'. Yet at the same time he is conscious of belief being at the basis of all serious poetry—and poetry not only of the religious past but also (with the examples of Yeats and D. H. Lawrence before him) very much of the present. During the course of the essay occur some of his celebrated grapplings with the problem of approaching poetry whose beliefs we feel to be ludicrous or outmoded or erroneous. Accordingly, he's led to his theory of what he calls the 'pseudo-statement'. He says: 'It is *not* the poet's business to make true statements. Yet poetry has constantly the air of making statements, and important ones; which is one reason why some mathematicians cannot read it. They find the alleged statements to be *false*.' Richards then goes on to argue that our acceptance of statements in poetry—pseudo-statements—is entirely governed by their effects on our feelings and attitudes. 'Logic only comes in, if at all, in subordination . . . to our emotional response.' Thus the statement in a poem 'is "true" if it suits and serves some attitude or links together attitudes which on other grounds are desirable. This kind of truth is so opposed to scientific "truth" that it is a pity to use so similar a word.'

One sees that this view of truth in poetry gets over two apparent difficulties. The first is a difficulty I've never myself been able to see as such. It's analogous to the kind of problem that so trivially, in many respects, bothered Bertrand Russell—the problem that one raises by adumbrating a piece of paper on one side of which is written the words: 'The statement on the other side of this paper is false'; and on the other side 'The statement on the other side of this paper is true'. Richards's own example, in the passage from which I've been quoting, of a poetic statement which must be a pseudo-statement and not a logical one is 'O Rose, thou art sick!' No doubt there is a convention that we must accept to go further into the poem (that a mathematician—or a plumber, for that matter—might not accept) in the business of addressing a flower (though to take the addressee as a girl called Rose will not throw the literally-minded amiss), but it is a quite rational cultural consequence, like the convention that used to exist of tipping one's hat as one passed the Cenotaph in Whitehall. If it is objected that there is something absurd or pathetically fallacious in attributing sickness to a flower, the answer is that an actual disease of the rose was undoubtedly intended to be conveyed by Blake, and further that 'the invisible worm' which later in the poem is educed as the disease's agent, has taken on a fresh dimension with the discovery of virus causation of plant disease. As for the poet's further intention that the rose shall stand for love or the female genitalia, I see no more logical crux in this than the mathematician telling us that A is to represent one of the apexes of an equilateral triangle.

One might add here (though perhaps not strictly on the point, and harking back to the idea of the scientific as the intrinsically poetic) that poets are more concerned with accuracy than many critics seem to allow. In 'The Palace of Art', a poem that Tennyson wrote in 1831 and 1832, he had the line 'She saw the snowy poles of moonless Mars'. (Strictly, the line appeared in some additional stanzas which Tennyson appended to the poem in a note in the 1832 edition—stanzas which he would have inserted if the poem, as he said, 'were not already too long'.) When the two satellites of Mars were discovered in 1877, Tennyson altered the line to 'She saw the snowy poles and Moons of Mars'. The astronomer Patrick Moore has recently reminded us (*Listener*, 30 July 1970) that even the revised line is wrong, for it's unlikely that the poles of Mars are snow-covered. So the line should now read 'She saw the snowless poles and Moons of Mars'. I feel sure that Tennyson's forced revision seemed to him to destroy some of the effect of the line—'Moons of Mars' is not only less euphonious than 'moonless Mars', it is also less strikingly particular. The further forced revision I've suggested—'snowless poles'—restores some of the original punch of the line in these regards.

The other so-called difficulty that the theory of the pseudo-statement may be thought to overcome is the element of the plainly wrong-headed or dotty in a poet's work. With Yeats and D. H. Lawrence in his mind, Richards obviously felt this as a particularly acute difficulty. But it seems to me to be one that has been exaggerated. It would be outside the scope of these remarks to try to justify my notion that the statements in poetry referable to factual or historical or, indeed, scientific conditions don't require a special dispensation from sense and accuracy. The Marxist critic Plekhanov had a useful phrase that the value of a work of art was, in the last analysis, determined by the specific gravity of its content. Certainly there is a happy tendency for art to sink into oblivion that runs counter to man's true needs and interests. And just to take the case of Yeats, the authoritarian side of him we know from his letters, the obscurantist side displayed in his prose book *A Vision*, have been too freely, I believe, extrapolated into his poetry. What we get from the poetry is much more neutral and sensible in these areas. I'm not, by using such terms, intending to play down the passion with which his ideas are presented, but simply making the point that his interest having been aroused, for example, in the cycles of social and political organization in civilizations, when he comes to work that interest out in his verse, he is, because he's a great and good poet, constantly referring it to true experience rather than letting it float fantastically free as in his prose speculations and in his studies.

I feel, in fact, that Richards's theory of the pseudo-statement is too modest. When he says that in the poetic approach logic enters only occasionally or not at all, one guesses that he is writing from an experience of poetry overwhelmingly of the Romantic kind— and quite substantially of the dilute romanticism that dominated the verse of the early part of this century, the verse which Richards would read with special interest as a boy and young man, for the poets of the dawn of the Romantic Movement would have been astonished to be told that their poetic statements were in any sense not true. I think the same experience colours the earlier arguments of *Science and Poetry*: for example, where Richards says that 'misunderstanding and underestimation of poetry is mainly due to over-estimation of the thought in it . . . It is never what a poem *says* which matters, but what it *is*. The poet is not writing as a scientist.'

Ironically, only two or three years after the publication of *Science and Poetry* the coming Thirties writers took up the poet for whom, above all, truth and the statement in their ordinary senses were important, Wilfred Owen. 'The true Poets must be truthful,' he said in his famous Preface. The Thirties confirmed and extended Owen's conviction that poetry had a use not merely in Arnold's spiritual sense or Richards's psychological sense but also, perhaps primarily, simply because poets were an articulate element in the State committed to no cause but the cause of truth. Their poems constituted warnings, messages, revelations, which philosophers, economists and statesmen were too blinkered, corrupt or timid to utter. This idealism about the poet's role seems to me not entirely misplaced. Poets are no stronger than other men but in their art must eschew compromise, must avoid avoidance, cannot fudge conclusions. The parallel with science is obvious. Both poetry and science are international. Both poets and scientists may be tempted or bullied into distortions of their discipline through national and commercial interests. But it's not too much to say (and I realize the philosophical pitfalls in trying to set up absolutes) that there are in science and poetry standards of truth that can't be abandoned and that essentially have never been abandoned.

In Richards's *Science and Poetry* there are some suggestive though by no means clear and logical remarks about the scientist's relation to poetry and science's effect on poetry. A few young scientists, Richards says, are free from accepting emotive utterances (such as poetry's pseudo-statements) as though they were established facts. Their responses thus remain undebilitated. But it is just these people who as a rule pay no serious attention to poetry. On the other hand, Richards seems to regard with dismay the effect which this neutral view of nature will have on poetry. 'Consider,' he says, 'the probable effects upon love-poetry in the near future of the kind of enquiry into basic human constitution exemplified by psychoanalysis.' What Richards seems to be advocating, then, is that the scientist (or anyone convinced of the neutrality of nature) shall accept poetry by training himself to suspend his disbelief in its pseudo-statements. And poetry itself will therefore have no need to do what Richards considers it congenitally unfitted to do—absorb such so-called neutralizing influences as psycho-analysis. If ever there was a twin recipe for alienating good readers and strangulating good poetry this, it seems to me, is it. Indeed, one often thinks anti-science equals bad poetry. 'All past consciousness is bunk. We're in science-fiction now . . . we're

back to magic.' One isn't surprised to find those the reported
words of Allen Ginsberg.

I find especially comic the notion that psychoanalysis might
somehow be inimical to poetry. The writings of the psycho-
analysts (let alone their excursions into applied psychoanalysis)
seem to be full of insights valuable to poetry. Despite Auden,
perhaps poetry has so far merely skirted round the fringes of the
subject. If I may mention my own case, I've sometimes done little
more than versify psychoanalytic points—the osmotic sap or huge
udder syndrome—and yet a few poems and individual lines I
count successful, and perhaps these still await their informed
readers.

Of course, it's in the university that the consanguinity of science
and poetry, of scientist and poet, of which I've been far too
sketchily speaking should above all be demonstrated. George
Steiner is one of the few academics or literary critics who clearly
perceive the unity of culture, and writing sympathetically but
acutely not long ago (*Cambridge Review*, 30 January 1970) about
the case of Leavis and of Leavis's case for the primacy of the
English School he was led into some remarks which admirably
embody what I would wish to say in relinquishing my subject
(relinquishing it at any rate for the time being).

It may be [said Dr Steiner] that crucial energies of spirit,
crucial vitalities of understanding have shifted, are shifting,
from the traditional arts to the sciences. It may be that non-
linguistic expressive codes—music, symbolic logic, mathematics—are taking on exploratory, life-giving and ordering
functions carried, hitherto, mainly by language. The whole
question is extremely complex and it affects almost every part
of our current lives ... Whether anyone not himself trained in
a scientific discipline will contribute anything conclusive (as
distinct from 'suggestive') to the whole argument is not certain.
Whether there can be real 'culture', in a sense both Leavis and
I would concur in, if the 'language-arts' ... lost their centrality
—is a very urgent, open question. But even to ask it clearly,

requires a genuine personal awareness—metaphoric as it must be to the mathematical illiterate—of the kinds of creative being, of shaping consciousness, now so deeply at work in the sciences.

Dr Steiner went on to say that Cambridge was 'one of the places in which the question can be most naturally posed' because of that university's current achievements in both molecular biology and astro-physics.

A seventeenth century sensibility [he added] would discern in this parallel brilliance of micro- and macroscopic discovery and model-building an absolutely central, somehow 'pre-destined' conjunction of spiritual energies—of energies that are philosophic and poetic in the deepest sense. In Cambridge intellectual but also moral adventures of a very strenuous, humanly-transforming order are being initiated and experienced. Can literary studies in any responsible way relate to this activity? . . . Are there conceivable ways in which the linguistic and moral sciences can offer any ground for collaborative interpenetration between those poetic modes of action proper to literature and those operative in the natural sciences? Coleridge . . . was certain of it. So, in very different senses, were Donne and, I would want to argue from the discipline of exact perception in his letters, Hopkins.

Obviously the scientific yeast is bubbling in Oxford, no less; and though historically Oxford literature is not Cambridge literature there is really no reason why it shouldn't now confront itself with the problems Dr Steiner outlined. I wouldn't want, even if I were qualified, to put the question in his high and dramatic terms, nor with quite the length of his perspectives. But who can doubt, when the best poets lack as well as conviction, amplitude and organization, and the worst only think themselves full of a passionate intensity, that it is high time that young poets attempted interpenetration (as the phrase goes) not only with the natural sciences but also, and consequentially, with a wider and realler world?

III

The Orbicularity of Bulbs

When I prepared my last lecture on poetry and science called 'The Osmotic Sap' I'd completely forgotten that in the year of his death Aldous Huxley had published a little book called *Literature and Science* which, moreover, summed up a whole life-time's interest in the subject, an interest which his remarkable ancestry very naturally gave him. I was reminded of the book and of the interest by the appearance, early this year of 1970, of the first collected edition of Huxley's poems. He was by no means an outstanding or significant poet but he devoted a great deal of time and energy to poetry during his initial period as a writer from the middle of the First World War to the end of the Twenties. And it's interesting to discover from his *Letters* that he was reading Jules Laforgue as early as 1915. This seems to have slightly predated his reading of, and friendship with, T. S. Eliot, though such historico-literary pronouncements can't be made with any dogmatism so long after the event and it's quite possible that the interest in Laforgue came in fact from Eliot.

What is beyond question is that Huxley's reading of the French symbolists didn't result in or contribute to, as it did in the cases of

Eliot and Wallace Stevens, a fresh concept of poetic diction. Perhaps the missing element in his early poetic education was reading or, more important, knowing Ezra Pound (though the imagination boggles at the result of the conjunction of the two personalities). Huxley, as an Oxford undergraduate, inherited the smooth Parnassianism of the Nineties and, though his verse got stronger, more sophisticated and more accomplished during the decade and a half when he practised it, it never really lost as one of its chief aims the resounding poetic 'touchstone'—to use the term invented by his great-uncle, Matthew Arnold. The novelty of Huxley's poetry is in its deliberate attempt to enlarge its scope by importing vocabulary, ideas and information from science and other disciplines.

The business forms the theme of two early essays—'Subject Matter of Poetry' in *On the Margin* (1923) and ' "And Wanton Optics Roll the Melting Eye" ' in *Music at Night* (1931). In the first of these essays Huxley draws attention to poetry's 'curiously narrow range of subject-matter'. Even modern poetry, which claims to have enlarged the bounds of poetry, has only returned to the moving facts of everyday life from 'the jewelled exquisiteness of the eighteen-nineties', is merely doing again what Homer and Chaucer did. Few poets have ever felt or now feel passionately about ideas and about strange remote facts, as does the scientist or the philosopher. 'The twentieth century still awaits its Lucretius, awaits its own philosophical Dante, its new Goethe, its Donne, even its up-to-date Laforgue. Will they ever appear? Or are we to go on producing a poetry in which there is no more than the dimmest reflection of that busy and incessant intellectual life which is the characteristic and distinguishing mark of this age?'

In the second essay Huxley returns to the notion that good scientific poetry is only possible where science has modified the 'existence-pattern' of the poet and so may be expected to modify the reader's existence-pattern, and again he singles out the poets mentioned in the previous essay as poets who have successfully done this. He contrasts them with didactic poets like Erasmus Darwin whose science has not modified their existence-patterns and whose rhymed botany and geology is essentially ridiculous.

It's a pity Huxley didn't take properly into account what had happened to English poetry between the dates of the two essays. He does, in the *Literature and Science* book of 1963, in a rapid survey of the forty years which had elapsed since he had first written on the subject matter of poetry, mention William Empson as the author of some elegant Neo-Metaphysical poetry. But he doesn't weigh Empson (or Michael Roberts, Charles Madge and others) whose existence-patterns in the late Twenties and early Thirties were distinctly modified by science, or at worst produced didactic verse. Nor, astonishingly enough, does he deal with W. H. Auden, whom the *zeistgeist* might have deliberately produced to answer Huxley's question of 1923 as to when the new Lucretius or whoever was going to appear. Huxley conventionally thinks of the Thirties as an age of 'social poetry'. Like so many of us, he was never adequately possessed of contemporary poetry later than that of his own youth.

We can't help feeling that his dismissal of a poet such as Erasmus Darwin was an inappropriate hangover from an epoch of too restricted a conception of what was proper in poetry: it is a reflection of the contradiction in Huxley's own verse between, on the one hand, the ironical aim and learned vocabulary, and, on the other, the rather consciously beautiful line of stiff poetic diction. There is amusing evidence of this hangover, which I've pointed out before, in the 1930 anthology of bad verse, *The Stuffed Owl*, which actually contains passages from many poets of the past (like Erasmus Darwin) who were coming to be admired. The whole business is brilliantly illustrated by the anthologies made later by one of the foremost entrepreneurs of Thirties poetry, Geoffrey Grigson, the anthologies he called *The Romantics* and *Before the Romantics*. One need only instance his rediscovery of the early eighteenth century poet William Diaper:

> *Strange the Formation of the Eely Race,*
> *That knows no Sex, yet loves the close Embrace.*

Their folded Lengths they round each other twine,
Twist am'rous Knots, and slimy Bodies joyn;
Till the close Strife brings off a frothy Juice,
The Seed that must the wriggling Kind produce.
Regardless they their future Offspring leave,
But porous Sands the spumy Drops receive.
That genial Bed impregnates all the Heap,
And little Eelets soon begin to creep.

Despite all Huxley said as a critic and all he tried to do as a
poet, we may feel that he always aimed instinctively to express a
notion of beauty in poetry which he had inherited; that fundamentally he placed didactic poetry, as did the Victorians, on a
lower level than poetry recognizably high-flown.

Huxley borrowed the title of his book *Literature and Science*
from that of the Rede Lecture that Matthew Arnold delivered
at Cambridge in 1882, and the book begins with a discussion of
the controversy concerning the 'two cultures' which was initiated
by C. P. Snow in the Rede Lecture given seventy-seven years
after Arnold's. Huxley tries, in the first part of his book, to contrast the aims and methods of the literary artist and the man of
science. It's curious how, starting off with superficial dissimilarities,
he's led in the end to discover likenesses. First, he says, science is a
device for investigating 'the more public of human experiences'.
Literature's main concern 'is with man's more private experiences'
—though it also deals with public experiences. Again, Huxley's
attempted contrast between the ways science and literature proceed from the particular to the general ends, really, by convincing
us that there is more similarity here than contrast. When he turns
to the question of language he says that as a medium of both
literary and scientific expression common language is inadequate.
Both the scientist and the literary artist need to 'give a purer
sense to the words of the tribe'. But, Huxley says, whereas the
scientist aims to speak unambiguously and with the greatest
possible clarity, that is not the aim of the literary artist, who puri-
fies 'not by simplifying and jargonizing, but by deepening and

extending, by enriching with allusive harmonies, with overtones of association and undertones of sonorous magic.'

Isn't, one feels, Huxley cheating here, and isn't he also advancing an altogether too romantic a view of literary language? People have often asked me whether my long stint as a lawyer wasn't particularly at odds with my simultaneous life as a poet, particularly in this field of the use of words. The answer is that in the quest for precision of expression and the excitement of the chase there is a good deal of common ground in drafting a poem and drafting a legal document. If further pressed, one must admit that though ideally a legal document should be free from what lawyers call latent and patent ambiguities, such an obligation does not weigh equally on the poem—at least, so far as patent ambiguity is concerned, the ambiguity that may reside in the very words of the poem itself. But does even this admission imply any great contradiction? William Empson has made poets as well as readers very knowing about poetic ambiguity, and one would guess that since 1930 (the date of publication of the Seven Types) poets have often spotted their ambiguities in the course of composition and have been pleased rather than otherwise. However, does any decent poet actually compose with the achieving of ambiguity in mind? I doubt it. One would say that his aim is, as it has always been, 'to speak unambiguously and with the greatest possible clarity'—the very phrase used by Huxley to characterize the aim of the scientist.

Then Huxley has a witty page or two on the poet's and the scientist's views of a flower. He quotes a botanical description of *Narcissus Pseudo-Narcissus*, including the words: 'The bulbs are large and orbicular.' Huxley continues: 'The primary interest of the literary artist is not in cells or genes or chemical compounds, not in the orbicularity of bulbs or the number of stamens ... His concern is with his own and other people's more private experiences in relation to flowers and with the multiple meanings he finds in them.' As to 'orbicularity', one could wish that Huxley's own verse had exploited more the ironical and arresting

possibilities of such vocabulary: intellectually and tempera-
mentally he was well equipped to do so.

> *That glabrous dome that lifts itself so grand,*
> *There in the marish, is the omphalous,*
> *The navel, umbo, middle, central boss*
> *Of the unique, sole, true Cloud-Cuckoo Land.*

We may feel that such lines are Huxley's true poetic vein and
that there are far too few of them. And thinking of the accuracy
of description inherent in such a word as 'orbicularity', we
remember how much of the poetry of the past survives through
that kind of particularity. Today, one of Browning's most admired poems is his 'Two in the Campagna' and I believe it has
attained that position simply through the vivid and curious detail
of its central image:

> *. . . First it left*
> *The yellowing fennel, run to seed*
> *There, branching from the brickwork's cleft,*
> *Some old tomb's ruin: yonder weed*
> *Took up the floating weft,*
>
> *Where one small orange cup amassed*
> *Five beetles,—blind and green they grope*
> *Among the honey-meal . . .*

I think, too, that something goes amiss in the next section of
Huxley's little book, where he is making the point that scientific
theories have a built-in obsolescence, so that if we still read Donne
it is for his language and his expression of timeless private experiences, and in despite of his knowledgeableness about pre-
Copernican astronomy and pre-Harveian physiology; and so,
too, it is the very precision of Dante's cosmology that is a barrier
to his modern readers. This is somewhat obvious—indeed,
dubious—stuff: more to the point would have been a consideration of how far such intellectual interests in Dante and Donne

were evidence of their being types of poets whose work has survived so long. Again, it's rather contradictory and weak of Huxley to add that the modern poet should take account of science because he isn't anyway writing for posterity, and because, too, the discoveries of modern science are likely to remain valid for far longer than Dante's septentrions and Donne's trepidations.

I was amused to find at the end of the Huxley book this phrase: 'The world is poetical intrinsically, and what it means is simply itself.' Amused and disconcerted, for I'd said, in my previous lecture, 'there is something almost intrinsically poetic in the scientific'. This is a notion I've been hawking round for years, imagining it to be my own property. But I think Huxley is expressing the same notion.

He closes his argument by speaking of the fascinating problem confronting the contemporary man of letters, 'the problem of harmonizing, within a single work of art, the old, beloved raw materials, handed down to him by the myth-makers of an earlier time, with the new findings and hypotheses now pouring in upon him from the sciences of his own day'. And he takes the case of the nightingale—the myth of Philomel and the marvellous melody in a world where chemical sprays destroy the bird's food, where the song is known to be a territorial claim and cyclical glandular changes bring silence to the singer which, contrary to the myth, is the cock-bird. The modern literary work, says Huxley, must be 'capable of expressing simultaneously the truth about nightingales, as they exist in their world of caterpillars, endocrine glands and territorial possessiveness, and the truth about the human beings who listen to the nightingale's song. It is a strangely complex truth about creatures who can think of the immortal bird in strictly ornithological terms and who at the same time are overcome (in spite of the ornithology, in spite of the ineradicable dirtiness of their ears) by the magical beauty of that plaintive anthem.'

No doubt there is about all this the ingenious simplicity, the superficial glitter, so characteristic of the conversation in Aldous Huxley's fiction—the speaker might be one of the reptilian old men in his novels of the Twenties. Thinking of the sophisticated literary criticism of today we may rightly feel that poets don't work in the way Huxley envisages. All the same one salutes him for hanging on to the faith in science of his grandfather's generation, all the more so when one thinks of the preoccupation with mysticism he acquired in middle-age, and the interest in hallucinatory drugs of his final years. For we must agree with the Marxists that quite often—and here I quote a phrase from Christopher Caudwell's *Studies in a Dying Culture*—'to the bourgeois . . . art and science appear not as creative opposites but as eternal antagonists'.

The quotation comes from the chapter on 'Beauty' in that characteristic book of the Thirties, and Caudwell, identifying science with truth, art with beauty, goes on to say that even Keats who saw the kinship of the two 'could yet complain that science had robbed the rainbow of its beauty'. This is because, Caudwell argues, art and science are seen by the bourgeois as things distinct, science situated entirely in the environment and art entirely in the heart. Of the two different worlds thus raised up, it is felt that one only can be chosen. But the one is bare of quality and the other destitute of reality, 'so that we cannot rest easily on either horn of the dilemma'. And he adds that 'the "secret" connection between the two is the world of concrete society'.

In the apocalyptic atmosphere of the Thirties Caudwell was too apt to bring his arguments to a conclusion by invoking the healing power of a society transformed by a proletarian revolution. No doubt that is a fault of most Marxist aestheticians. But more than most Caudwell throws out some suggestive remarks on the way. I like particularly his description of how the social process of living increases the exploration of outer reality and how that exploration alters the nature of inner desire.

This pressure [he says] both in science and art, appears as an individual experience. A scientist inherits the hypotheses, and an artist inherits the traditions, of the past. In the scientist's case an experiment, and in the artist's case a vital experience indicates a discrepancy, a tension, whose synthesis results in a new hypothesis or a new art work. Of course the scientist feels the tension as an error, as something in the environment; the artist as an urge, as something in his heart.

Caudwell's appeal to tradition here, as well as his parallels between literary and scientific creativity, would be found strange, I dare say, by most so-called revolutionary poets of the present. The appeal resembles T. S. Eliot's. What is new in Caudwell, and characteristically of the Thirties, is the unselfconscious way that for him poetry is open to science, allied with science. It is a thing that comes out in his own poetry, not so much in lines like his image for a skeleton, 'The white and knobbled chassis of the flesh', as in whole passages where he obviously feels free to express both sides of his nature, the literary and the scientific. One doesn't want to claim too much for Caudwell as a poet, particularly as against other poets of the Thirties who possessed wide interests and felt a similar freedom. But I think he does, looking at him all round, represent something that had returned to poetry after a very long absence: one couldn't make about him such a remark as Huxley in *Literature and Science* makes about Eliot, that 'From a reading of "The Waste Land" and "Sweeney Among the Nightingales" one would never suspect that he was a contemporary of Eliot Howard and Konrad Lorenz.' Eliot himself called for a poet to have wide interests and was ideologically prepared for such interests appearing in a poet's verse, but we may think the faint alarm he expressed when specifically encountering them was not altogether humorous and ironic. 'With Shelley,' he said in *The Use of Poetry and the Use of Criticism*, 'we are struck from the beginning by the number of things poetry is expected to do; from a poet who tells us, in a note on vegetarianism, that "the orang-outang perfectly resembles man both in the order and the number of his teeth", we shall not know what not to expect.'

In this and my previous lecture on poetry and science I'm very conscious that the discussion may have been too naïve both for those interested in science and those interested in poetry. Even worse, I'm well aware that there are conclusions to be drawn that I'm not capable of extracting. The early Romantic poets proclaimed an emotional relationship with science—or perhaps renewed it, for the attitude has something in common with that of poets of the seventeenth century. But the very intensity of the emotion implied the quite rapid disillusion—in Keats, in the later Wordsworth, to say nothing of the lesser Romantics of the middle part of the nineteenth century, there is a strong anti-scientific temper. When the modern movement in poetry begins this ambivalence towards science is immediately characteristic. Michael Hamburger has pointed out, in his fascinating book *The Truth of Poetry*, how Baudelaire could within a few years express both points of view. In 1852 he said: 'The time is not distant when it will be understood that all literature which refuses to march fraternally between science and philosophy is a homicidal or suicidal literature.' In 1859 he said: 'Death or deposition would be the penalty if poetry were to become assimilated to science or morality; the object of poetry is not truth, the object of poetry is Poetry itself.' We are apt to think of Baudelaire as the embodiment of this latter attitude, the precursor of the vast amount of modern poetry that has fed on itself and been reckless in its esotericism, but Mr Hamburger reminds us that as a critic he by no means concentrated 'on the aesthetic and stylistic aspects of a poem' but was 'concerned with the public functions of the arts as much as with their inner laws'—had more in common, in fact, with Matthew Arnold than with Poe or Mallarmé.

One's tempted to say that despisal or fear of science has been a characteristic of developments in modern poetry when such developments have become impossibly inbred. I draw again on Mr Hamburger's wide knowledge and perception, his account, in an essay called 'Brecht and his Successors' (*Review*, No. 24), of Brecht's attempt 'to "wash" the language of poetry'—'what he washed out of poetry was nothing less than the sediment of the whole Romantic-Symbolist era, with its aesthetic of self-sufficiency'. As Mr Hamburger says, Brecht's purpose was closely connected with his Marxist beliefs, including the notion that the Romantic-Symbolist aesthetic was the outcome of bourgeois individualism, but I think his motivation can be understood quite apart from his political experience or social purpose. Brecht is an extreme case of a good many modern poets who come to strive for a less figurative language, a simpler metric; to renounce vague and emotive effects; to delineate the world rather than themselves. To quote Mr Hamburger once more:

> What Brecht wanted . . . was a social poetry of dialogue about matters of interest to everyone. This eminently classical relationship between writer and reader had long been made impossible by the individualism of writers and readers alike, and nowhere more so than in serious and advanced poetry, with its need to escape from vulgar norms of communication in every conceivable direction. Brecht, therefore, undertook a drastic and rigorous revision of the function of poetry and of poets so as to put both back where he thought they belonged, in society and in history.
>
> ('Brecht and his Successors')

There's more than a touch of the bathetic in setting against this the aims of the romantic poets who flourished in England at the end of the Thirties and in the early Forties, the poets who called themselves the Apocalyptics. But though their work may not have amounted to much, the attitude behind it was of more than temporary significance. Here is a passage from the 1941 anthology of the movement, *The White Horseman* (it is from an essay by G. S. Fraser and is quoted by John Press in his *A Map of Modern English Verse*):

> The discoveries of Freud, and the work of the Surrealists . . . have convinced the Apocalyptics that every poet has enough to write about in the contents of his own mind, and that the struggle to be classic, social, relevant, and so on, is unnecessary; because if a poet describes honestly his private perspective in

the world, his private universe, human minds are sufficiently analogous to each other for that private universe to become (ultimately though certainly not immediately) a generally accessible human property.

A similar attitude, taken to an absurder extreme, is seen at the present time. Allen Ginsberg, for instance, has been reported to have said: 'We're in science-fiction now . . . we're back to magic . . . all public reality's a script, and anybody can write the script the way he wants.' (See *Paterfamilias: Allen Ginsberg in America* by Jane Kramer.)

Without the scientific respect for and examination of reality any poetic movement towards colloquialism of diction or freedom of form seems doomed to end in mere rhetoric or sentimentality or vapidity. Surely this partly accounts for the artistic failure of many young poets of today who may otherwise have decent notions of poetry being accessible, part of everyday life, the art not of a class or of an élite. Moreover, the poetry of a private world is all too apt to turn into a poetry that encourages a reactionary public world. The extreme violence, of imagery and ideas, of some contemporary poetry goes beyond any attempt to depict, to grapple with, our present woes: it seems likely, rather, to add to those woes by providing their mere artistic mimicry. I've never been able to see why art, in the face of chaos, feels that it must itself be chaotic. No doubt the public events we have lived through have given many poets such an acute sense of urgency that they have been led into raw messages, have often been dissuaded from elaborate or prolonged works. But the task of ordering reality remains. Even one of the most apparently obscure, most superficially mandarin of modern poets, Wallace Stevens, remarked that 'the philosophy of the sciences is not opposed to poetry', and again: 'Is not the concept of final knowledge poetic?'

One must go on to add that despite one's sympathy with the Brechtian cleansing process, no simplification of the means of poetry should renounce the complications of reality. Any poet who heard or read H. A. Mason's lectures on *Pope and Homer* given in this university in 1969 must have been enormously struck by this aspect of Pope's art that came out of them. Wordsworth said of both Pope and Dryden that they 'could habitually think that the visible universe was of so little consequence to a Poet, that it was scarcely necessary for him to cast his eye upon it'. Later, Coleridge reinforced this view by examining, in the *Biographia Literaria*, a passage from Pope's translation of Homer. It is Mr Mason's case that the arguments of Wordsworth and Coleridge have met with little opposition because of the practice of publishing Pope's translation without his Notes.

Until I read the Notes [Mr Mason said], I thought Pope had no eyes for Nature, and so I gave up the effort to make anything of the translations. But when (I must state with bitterness) in late middle-age I first used Pope's original edition, I found the Notes abounding in *absolute proof* that Pope had the keenest eye for large and small natural effects, and that he considered possession of a similar eye as one of Homer's greatest gifts.

I should like to quote just one example which Mr Mason gives in support of his case. Here is a passage from the Fifth Book of the *Iliad* in Mr Mason's own literal translation:

> But the soldiers had no need of this; they
> Shewed no fear as they faced the expected charge of the Trojans.
> They stood firm and still like clouds which the son of Chronos
> Halts over mountain peaks when the air is calm and unmoving,
> Motionless in the sleep of the North Wind's fury and all wild
> Winds that storm and blow their cold shrill breath to a whistle,
> And scatter and drive off the clouds that cover the mountains with
>   shadows.
> So the Greeks stood firm and still and awaited the Trojans.

Now here is Pope's translation:

The fiercest Shock of charging Hosts sustain;

Unmov'd and silent, the whole War they wait,
Serenely dreadful, and as fix'd as Fate.
So when th'embattl'd Clouds in dark Array
Along the Skies their gloomy Lines display,
When now the North his boisterous Rage has spent,
And peaceful sleeps the liquid Element,
The low-hung Vapors, motionless and still,
Rest on the Summits of the shaded Hill;
'Till the Mass scatters as the Winds arise,
Dispers'd and broken thro' the ruffled Skies.

In his Notes Pope remarks that the beauty and aptness of this simile may be lost on many readers because it is a description of a natural appearance they may never have had a chance of seeing.

It happens frequently in very calm Weather [Pope continues], that the Atmosphere is charg'd with thick Vapors, whose Gravity is such, that they neither rise nor fall, but remain poiz'd in the Air at a certain Height, where they continue frequently for several Days together. In a plain Country this occasions no other visible Appearance but of an uniform clouded Sky; but in a Hilly Region these Vapors are to be seen covering the Tops and stretch'd along the Sides of the Mountains, the clouded Parts above being terminated and distinguish'd from the clear Parts below by a strait Line running parallel to the Horizon, as far as the Mountains extend.

Pope even goes on to justify out of nature the scattering part of the simile which, as Mr Mason remarks, we can't believe was Homer's own intention.

I've no time to more than mention Mr Mason's deeper thesis here, which is Augustan art's remaking of Nature as Fact into Nature as Value. What's germane to my own more modest theme is the striking confirmation that a poet so acute about human nature could, if that had been his purpose, have been just as acute in his verse about the natural world. It's perhaps something we could have guessed from our sense of the marvellous alertness of

Pope's entire poetic work, but it is good to have the thing made so concrete.

The richness and unity of English intellectual life is not, of course, confined to the Augustan age. Those qualities go back to Elizabethan and Jacobean times and, despite crisis and strain, forward to the high Victorian years. No doubt increasing specialization has stretched the fabric thin, but both scientists and poets have, it seems to me, too easily renounced interest in each other's doings. The papers of Thomas Harriot (only now being thoroughly investigated) show how the scientist's interests in the age of Shakespeare extended to language and the practical affairs of man. In the late seventeenth century the scientific activities of a figure like Edmond Halley have a strong air of poetic discovery, as one sees if one simply lists some of the papers he wrote or published in 1691—'An Account of the Circulation of the watry Vapours of the Sea'; 'A Discourse tending to prove at what time and place, Julius Caesar made his first descent upon Britain'; 'A Way of Estimating the Necessary Swiftness of the Wings of Birds to sustain their Weight in the Air'; and papers discussing the sun's distance, the refraction of light, and the height to which fountains could be made to operate. We must feel that Darwin and Huxley, Tennyson and Arnold, are much more at arms' length, but perhaps not until the end of the nineteenth century was the breach ignorable by poets, even thought to have positive advantages. When one comes in our own time to an extreme symbolist poet like Dylan Thomas, nature, ostensibly the subject of much of the poetry, is largely a mere series of pegs on which to hang words.

And one can't resist turning to another art for the example of what may be thought to be the ultimate in the artist's incomprehension and degradation of science—the modern sculptor's making of machines of no purpose, that don't work. Such insane abstractions from the true, the useful and the beautiful must be contrasted with the real things that have been produced by the scientist and the technician in every age—from Harriot's mathematical diagrams, through steam-driven engines, to the molecular models of our own times.

I'm sure that the sympathetic scientist would admit that the faults are not all on the side of art. Science in the service of profit-motivated industry, of the war-machine of the State; the scientist himself as a middlebrow or even a philistine in relation to the arts—all these serve, in their varyingly important ways, to perpetuate the two cultures. And I suspect that the division is drawn at a very early point in education, and continued throughout education, so that the English faculty library is as much a closed shop as some edifice round the corner by the Parks. The official attempts to heal the breach, though worthy, sometimes make me shudder. The humane studies foisted on scientists at student level must be of extremely variable value. A poet of today visits a college of technology to read his poems. What misunderstandings ensue, what wrong notions are accepted, what mutual stimulus missed? Both parties are likely to be wound in the cocoons of their specialized techniques and esoteric ambitions. Yet both parties have essentially the same purpose—the delineation and amelioration of the real world.

W. H. Auden (in his 'commonplace book', *A Certain World*) has recently added an amusing footnote to the controversy about the two cultures:

Of course [he said], there is only one. Of course, the natural sciences are just as 'humane' as letters. There are, however, two languages, the spoken verbal language of literature, and the written sign language of mathematics, which is the language of science. This puts the scientist at a great advantage, for, since like all of us he has learned to read and write, he can understand a poem or a novel, whereas there are very few men of letters who can understand a scientific paper once they come to the mathematical parts.

When I was a boy [Auden goes on to say], we were taught the literary languages, like Latin and Greek, extremely well, but mathematics atrociously badly. Beginning with the multiplication table, we learned a series of operations by rote which, if remembered correctly, gave the 'right' answer, but about any

basic principles, like the concept of number, we were told
nothing. Typical of the teaching methods then in vogue is this
mnemonic which I had to learn.

Minus times Minus equals Plus:
The reason for this we need not discuss.

Obviously in the last forty or fifty years the teaching of mathematics has improved, but whether any substantially better links
between science and letters have been made is more doubtful.
Early specialization is probably still a great evil. But worse, I
think, is the spurious romanticism of men of letters that refuses,
again in Auden's words, 'to sacrifice . . . aesthetic preference to
reality or truth . . . What the poet has to convey is not "self-
expression", but a view of reality common to all, seen from a
unique perspective, which it is his duty as well as his pleasure to
share with others.'

It would be more reassuring that such duty were to be performed if one were likely to find on a young poet's shelves a work
like James Newman's marvellous anthology *The World of Mathematics* rather than the prophetic books of this or any other age.
Even, one sometimes feels, the chopped-up prose that almost
universally serves today as poetic form arises from unconfidence
in the ability to count.

IV

The Two Sides of the Street

I've always felt the chief—or, at any rate, the initial—difficulty of the novel to be the question of the narrating consciousness. The problem is a familiar one to the student of Henry James, and I suppose it was from James that I remotely inherited it when I began to try my hand at prose fiction in my teens. I'd not then read James, nor were books and articles on James's technical side so abundant in those days of the nineteen-twenties, but the problem was obviously in the air, infecting all with serious ambitions in fiction, so that as one moved out of one's schoolboy imitations of Aldous Huxley one was laid low by the malady. It is a problem of getting verisimilitude, and therefore central to an art whose development has been towards greater sophistication while retaining, in general, its function of depicting human relations within society.

Quite early in his career James rejected the convention of authorial omniscience. That the puppets should be seen to be manipulated was utterly impermissible. But there is, of course, a more subtle point about authorial omniscience: it is that the author claims to be there on every occasion in the novel, to report what is being said and thought and done. This, also, with the increasing sophistication of the art comes to be seen as puppet-mastery of too blatant a kind. One alternative, which James seized on, is to select a character (or successive characters) through whose consciousness the action of the novel is depicted. A development of the device was to choose for this purpose a character not necessarily mainly involved in the action—a curious and sensitive observer.

I suppose one might think, if the business had remained theoretical, had not been actually written into the development of the novel over the last hundred years, that strictness about the viewpoint of narration was an entirely minor matter, of interest only to rather Byzantine practitioners of the art of fiction. After all, one might argue, since the main convention of fiction has never been seriously challenged—which is that the reader is going to interest himself in the affairs of imaginary people—it would seem scarcely to matter how those affairs were technically related. I mean that plot, characterization, observation, quality of writing, would seem to be factors overwhelmingly more important. Of course, one can see that it is risky for the author to keep reminding his audience that what they are reading is a figment of his imagination, but that apart one might conceive that the author had a free hand.

It's my feeling that his hands are in fact tied because the novel has taken over, during the period I've mentioned, some of the functions of other literary forms, poetry in particular. Naturally, I realize that the development of any art form is a complicated question, not to be accounted for in a few general phrases. The social question looms largely behind it, and it would be quite outside my powers and the scope of this lecture for me to say anything about the novel's changing audience, mode of dissemination and so forth. Nor can I do more than mention the new rivals and allies in the field of verisimilitude that have at once restricted and intensified the practice of novel-writing—the cinema, the microphone, the tape-recorder. Moreover, technical change in an art is usually initiated by the art's most talented practitioners, so that their successes are seen, are seized on, by the epigoni often

3

more as matters of technique than of a finer response to life. And thus technical change comes to have its own dynamism.

Before I return to the question of the novel and poetry I must say a word or two more about Henry James's technical precepts. It's interesting that as well as rejecting the method of authorial omniscience he also came to reject, except for the shorter fiction or the horror tale, first person narration—interesting and at first blush curious. For wouldn't one be inclined to think that to tell one's imaginary story in the first person would be to remove a layer of convention, would more easily induce the reader to accept that what he was reading was verisimilitudinous? Of course, it is incumbent on the author in that event to provide a narrator who may plausibly be conceived to be capable of putting down his 70,000 words or whatever; and also to provide an occasion, a motive, for the narrator doing that very thing. But the business is not too difficult, after all. The epistolary novel, for example, has a long and successful ancestry. The documentary confession following the more or less shattering events which the confession proposes to narrate is more essentially a convention, but by no means outside reasonable probability. And again, if the narrator is made to be a literary man or otherwise addicted to scribbling, or if the narration is cast in the form of an autobiography or autobiographical document, the novelist may feel himself to be home and dry in this particular form.

James recognized the persuasion and conviction residing in the first person method and, as I've said, did not wholly renounce it. But his suspicions of it were extremely suggestive and I shall want later on to try to see them in the light of the poet's experience. James has a phrase for the technique in his preface to *The Ambassadors*: 'the terrible fluidity of self-revelation'. Though I'm afraid I shall soon have to quote a lengthy passage from that preface, the whole piece should be read for the full and quite unparaphrasable account of James's scruples. The symmetry, the strictness of *The Ambassadors* required, in James's conception, a single narrative viewpoint, to wit, its hero's; but a viewpoint made rigorous by its being James himself, not the hero, who is to determine what the hero 'sees'. This isn't just a quibble, for James is not, finally, the hero, Strether; nor Strether James. The choice of the narrative method is also a question of the choice of tone; and the events of *The Ambassadors* come to us through Strether's eyes but tinted, magnified, selected, by James's own spectacles. Here, for example, is James on the problems he faced right at the start of the novel, the coming over of Strether from the United States, a passage which leads up to the phrase from the preface I've already quoted:

He arrives (arrives at Chester) as for the dreadful purpose of giving his creator 'no end' to tell about him—before which rigorous mission the serenest of creators might well have quailed. I was far from the serenest; I was more than agitated enough to reflect that, grimly deprived of one alternative or one substitute for 'telling', I must address myself tooth and nail to another. I couldn't, save by implication, make other persons tell *each other* about him—blest resource, blest necessity, of the drama, which reaches its effects of unity, all remarkably, by paths absolutely opposite to the paths of the novel: with other persons, save as they were primarily *his* persons (not he primarily but one of theirs), I had simply nothing to do. I had relations for him none the less, by the mercy of Providence, quite as much as if my exhibition *was* to be a muddle; if I could only by implication and a show of consequence make other persons tell each other about him, I could at least make him tell *them* whatever in the world he must; and could do so, by the same token—which was a further luxury thrown in—see straight into the deep differences between what that could do for me, or at all events for *him*, and the large ease of 'autobiography'. It may be asked why, if one so keeps to one's hero, one shouldn't make a single mouthful of 'method', shouldn't throw the reins on his neck and, letting them flap there as free as in *Gil Blas* or in *David Copperfield*, equip him with the double privilege of subject and object—a course that has at least the merit of brushing away questions at a sweep. The answer to which is, I think, that one makes that surrender only if one is prepared *not* to make certain precious discriminations.

The 'first person' then, so employed, is addressed by the author directly to ourselves, his possible readers, whom he has to reckon with, at the best, by our English tradition, so loosely and vaguely after all, so little respectfully, on so scant a presumption of exposure to criticism. Strether, on the other hand, encaged and provided for as 'The Ambassadors' encages and provides, has to keep in view proprieties much stiffer and more salutary than any our straight and credulous gape are likely to bring home to him, has exhibitional conditions to meet, in a word, that forbid the terrible *fluidity* of self-revelation.

One might add here a further objection to first-person narration of which the gaminess of James's late prose in this preface reminds us. The novelist using that method is strictly not only under the obligation of assuming a persona but also a style. I wasn't pleased when a reviewer in *The Times Literary Supplement* said about my novel *The Carnal Island* that the narrator there, while self-mocking about his prose style (which it is suggested he has caught from another character in the book), surely cannot be taken to be too serious about the point since his style is suspiciously like the style of Roy Fuller. However, though the objection is perhaps one which a good-natured and large-minded critic wouldn't think of making, it has substance.

Henry James reminds us, in the passage I've quoted, of the case of the drama. There, the authorial omniscience is entire—but it is completely acceptable at the price paid by the playwright of forbearing to enter the minds of his characters and to comment on their actions. And I must go on to say that dramatists who have been unwilling to sacrifice those privileges more proper to other forms of literary art seem to me to have put the drama in peril—one thinks of the characters' spoken thoughts in some plays by Eugene O'Neill and the alienation effects of Brecht. *Per contra*, modern novelists must often be tempted to regain the advantages of authorial omniscience by adopting the form of the drama, that is to say keeping their descriptions and psychological comments to a minimum—mere stage directions or hints to actors. The novels of

Ivy Compton-Burnett spring to mind in this connection. But there is a fundamental tendency to unreadableness about the text of a play, from which Ivy Compton-Burnett's fictions are not free. The drama has lessons for the novelist but not, I think, in this aspect of its technique. The lessons are rather those of economical construction and sharp confrontation which James himself learned from his tragicomic experiences in the theatre and which he put into practice in his last novels.

I want, conscious of the banality involved, to return to my own experience of the novelist's technical problems. I remember before the war being so captured by the notion of the single narrating consciousness that I could scarcely escape also from the obligation to keep the time scheme continuous, the consequence being not only a compressed action but also a large import into the fiction of the minute by minute details of human existence. Luckily little of this fiction saw the light of day. It derived, I would say, from the obsessive application of the single narrating consciousness known as the stream of consciousness technique: I'd read early on, with approval, the work of Dorothy Richardson and Virginia Woolf. Towards the end of the war, when a desk job in the Navy gave me the chance to practise prose fiction again, it seemed to me that I could only achieve any freedom of technique through the novel of action, and I wrote then an adventure story for children and, later, three novels of pursuit. The question of tone bothered me, too. I thought I might not be able to engage the interest of the adult intelligent reader; whereas I felt less daunted contemplating a public of children and addicts of the crime story.

Perhaps this enslavement by technical problems is only too characteristic of lack of genius, of which indeed I've always been acutely aware. But I'll pursue the business in the hope that it has, in fact, wider connotations. The parallels with the kind of poetry that poets in our time have been able to write seem to me to be interesting. The change in English poetry brought about by Eliot and Pound is usually thought to be chiefly concerned with diction and prosodic form. But I think what must strike one about Eliot's early verse is its escape from 'the terrible fluidity of self-revelation' (an escape which, as the drafts of 'The Waste Land' show, was abetted by Pound). In 'The Love Song of J. Alfred Prufrock' and 'Portrait of a Lady' there is a narrating consciousness but it is not that of the poet himself. In Pound's own case, the Browningesque device of the historical or fictional mask was an initial adoption, and was developed and refined through such books as *Cathay*.

The persona assumed by Eliot in his first poems, a persona middle-aged, ineffectual, sensitive but rather comic, is not only an escape from 'the terrible fluidity of self-revelation': it is a device that enables him to put into poetry an element missing from the etiolated verse of the post-Tennysonians. It is what I think of as 'the nose-picking element'. The notion comes from Henry Green's novel *Living*, where the hero picks his nose under cover of reading his engagement book, an incident which struck me greatly when I came across it in 1929. But of course it is an element much to the fore in the work of many novelists of that period, Aldous Huxley, for example, and I suppose it stems from *Ulysses*, the nose-picking novel supreme—indeed, nose-picking in the case of that work being very much a euphemism for other human activities. I thought, I think still, of this element as adding a good deal to fiction's verisimilitude, and also of constituting a counterpoint—a richness of depth and contrast—to the higher themes of life which the novel offers to delineate. In Eliot's early verse the nose-picking element is restrained (and perhaps one has now to make an historical effort of the imagination to recapture its force) but it is indubitably there:

> Time to turn back and descend the stair,
> With a bald spot in the middle of my hair—
> (They will say: 'How his hair is growing thin!')
> My morning coat, my collar mounting firmly to the chin,
> My necktie rich and modest, but asserted by a simple pin—
> (They will say: 'But how his arms and legs are thin!')

The masks assumed by Pound may be thought of rather as enabling him to escape from the poet's essential situation, which is the confrontation of the world by a contemplative and usually timid or deformed personality. I'm aware that with this rather drastic description I'm perhaps generalizing too freely from the experience of the poet in bourgeois society. In more primitive (and possibly in more advanced) communities the drawbacks of the poetic character were, and will be, sustained and valued by the sympathy and support of society at large. But the obsession with words and patterns, the concern with but essential irony about human endeavour, the continuous sense of a seductive but inimical natural world, does set the poet apart; and in lyrical poetry, poetry of direct confrontation between the world and the poet himself, there is a tendency to monotony and weakness that is bound to obtrude, a tendency more pronounced as the poet's strong youthful libido inevitably dies down. Undoubtedly the initial impulse of the poet is to test out, to exploit, his personal adolescent response to experience, but I have elsewhere called this kind of poetry 'the tyranny of the lyric "I"' and a tyranny I believe it to be or to become, one from which the poet must find a strategy to escape. Pound's strategies were various, none more remarkable than that which enabled him to publish during the First War a poem that begins like this:

While my hair was still cut straight across my forehead
I played about the front gate, pulling flowers.
You came by on bamboo stilts, playing horse,
You walked about my seat, playing with blue plums.
And we went on living in the village of Chokan:
Two small people, without dislike or suspicion.

At fourteen I married my Lord you.
I never laughed, being bashful.
Lowering my head, I looked at the wall.
Called to, a thousand times, I never looked back.

At fifteen I stopped scowling,
I desired my dust to be mingled with yours
For ever and for ever and for ever.

I deliberately mentioned the First War in connection with this

poem, for that event, it seems to me, not only obliged the poet
serving in it to submit to the tyranny of the lyric 'I'—it also
changed the nature of the tyranny by assimilating the poet's experience to that of his audience. Undoubtedly the crisis of the lyric
poet arises as well from the separateness of the literary life, a
separateness disguised (or not existing at all) in his youth, but
increasingly evidencing itself as the accumulation of a set of experiences more or less esoteric, of objective correlatives unshared
by his audience. In Wilfred Owen, in Siegfried Sassoon, the poetic
penetration and sensitivity pay dividends of a kind that had perhaps
not been received from poetry since the Romantic Revolution—
or, indeed, since poetry had been altogether more primitive and
utilitarian. They were able to interpret, tell the hidden truth about,
great and bewildering events in which men in general were
involved. It was as though poetry once more was helping men to
turn the capstan or pull in the catch.

There have been two interesting lines of criticism of the poetry
written by poets like Owen and Sassoon during the First War.
The one, voiced most notoriously by W. B. Yeats, is, as he said,
that 'passive suffering is not a theme for poetry'. The other is that
the war laid on the poet a duty to cast his experience not in personal
but in epic form. I want in a subsequent lecture to discuss these
questions, but I would briefly say now that my feeling is that the
nature of society's crisis revealed by the First War and the quality
of Owen's poetry in particular put that poetry, in a sense, out of
reach of criticism of that sort. On the other hand, when one comes
to the English poetry of the Second War one must admit that the
personal response was inadequate, and not so much because no
Owen was thrown up as because the event was generally understood, civilians and soldiers alike suffered and were without
illusion; patriotism and human sacrifice needed no puncturing or
illumination; and the longing for peace was present as the first
air-raid siren sounded. The 'I' in the poetry of the Second War is
too often simply one suffering nostalgia for a happy personal life
that was interrupted or made impossible of achievement by the
war.

The question also arises, considering more recent verse, of the validity of so-called 'confessional' poetry. Some such poetry, and I think particularly of a few of Robert Lowell's poems, would justify itself in a way similar to the poetry of the First War—that is to say, as the response, truthful in a unique way, of the poet to public events of an obscure and shattering kind. But by and large it is mania in the poet, not the world's mania, that is said to be the justification for confessional poetry. Alternatively (and this is seen today in what one thinks of as an extension of confessional poetry) the mania of the world is taken to be a justification for maniac poetry. I don't think I need to document extensively these kinds of poetry. In a sense all poetry, even Dryden's, is confessional, but the term has come to mean a direct and circumstantial admission of weakness and unbalance, while what I have called maniac poetry wouldn't, I think, allow itself very much internal order of syntax, imagery or thought. A few lines of each kind will remind you of the *genres*. Confessional:

Sleepmonger,
deathmonger,
with capsules in my palms each night,
eight at a time from sweet pharmaceutical bottles
I make arrangements for a pint-sized journey.
I'm the queen of this condition.

(Anne Sexton: 'The Addict')

Maniac:

The sky is myself and myself is lead and myself crushes
*   down on the soft soft neck of summer. I'll eat it.*
It's a secret. You're safe—hot gem/melt pearl, gone gob
*   of energy.*
It's prisoned palmed.
It'll poison my pocket.
The metal will kill down your dangerous prayers.

(Jeff Nuttall: 'Driving the jumper')

I think one can say about both these kinds of poetry that they are a reaction from the sober reporting of universal experience that is thought by some poets and critics to be part of an outworn tradition in English poetry. But both kinds, it seems to me, increase the tyranny of the personal pronoun. The confessional poet, to pursue the line most germane to my theme, is easily led into an embarrassing inflation of his emotions and situation. On the one hand sentimentality lurks; and on the other a sort of public relations presentation of character, a simultaneous simplification and exaggeration that calls to mind the presentation of so-called 'personalities' by media like the Sunday supplements and television. Any single example is perhaps invidious but the evolution of the American poet John Berryman* from the restrained writer he was in the Thirties may be mentioned, culminating—surely—in the recently-published book called *Love and Fame*. The megalomania of this work is not to be turned into something else by the author writing, for the English edition, an 'Afterword' explaining that the title is ironic and that the obsession with erotic encounters and public attention mere evidence of insecurity.

It seems not to be realized that the appearance of the poet himself in his poetry is a tricky business. It has to be underwritten by more than extreme experience or intense emotion. If one thinks of a personal poetry which is also great poetry, Yeats's later work, one sees at once how much of himself the poet has subsumed in causes greater than himself and also how much impersonal work is carried on in parallel. Self-indulgence is far from Yeats, both in aim and execution; and the personal elements of memory and situation are universalized by being attached to other people and to history.

Not long ago, in an excellent book about Henry James's craftsmanship called *The Expense of Vision* by Laurence Bedwell Holland, I came across what seemed to me a most striking phrase. It is this: Henry James 'was to insist . . . that the novel was the most intimate of forms'. I think the first reaction to this, particularly of the poet, must be to object, since that description seems surely to be reserved

* This passage was written before the poet's death and the publication of a further book, *Delusions, Etc.*

for the poem, or at any rate the lyrical poem. But an instant's reflection convinces one of the truth of the statement, paradoxical
though it may appear, and further pondering raises in vague but
strong form the whole of one's experience in the two activities of
poet and novelist.

Professor Holland takes as evidence for his pregnant observation
a remarkable lecture that Henry James delivered for the Royal
Society of Literature on the occasion of the centenary of Browning's birth in 1912. The lecture consists of a consideration of the
novelistic aspects of Browning's *The Ring and the Book* (it was
reprinted in James's critical book *Notes on Novelists*). In its severely
technical interests but highly metaphorical style the lecture has
obvious affinities with the prefaces James wrote for the New York
Edition of his own fiction, including the preface to *The Ambassadors* from which I quoted earlier. I'm afraid I must also quote
quite a large chunk of the lecture, for no summary can really do
justice to the subtle point James is making. The novelistic elements
in *The Ring and the Book*—the complications of the plot, the
number of characters, the successive strict narrating conscious-
nesses—involve us in the poem in such an urgent way that we have
to make a deliberate effort of detachment to experience it as a
poem. Nevertheless these elements are, for Browning, poetry;
and that is what makes *The Ring and the Book* so unusual a poem.
Here is James's key passage:

What remains with us all this time, none the less, is the effect of
magnification, the exposure of each of these figures, in its degree,
to that iridescent wash of personality, of temper and faculty,
that our author ladles out to them, as the copious share of each,
from his own great reservoir of spiritual health, and which
makes us, as I have noted, seek the reason of a perpetual anomaly.
Why, bristling so with references to *him* rather than with
references to each other or to any accompanying set of circumstances, do they still establish more truth and beauty than they
sacrifice, do they still, according to their chance, help to make
The Ring and the Book a great living thing, a great objective mass?

I brushed by the answer a moment ago, I think, in speaking of the development in Pompilia of the resource of expression, which brings us round, it seems to me, to the justification of Browning's method. To express his inner self—his outward was a different affair!—and to express it utterly, even if no matter how, was clearly, for his own measure and consciousness of that inner self, to *be* poetic; and the solution of all the deviations and disparities or, speaking critically, monstrosities, in the mingled tissue of this work, is the fact that whether or no by such convulsions of soul and sense life got delivered for him, the garment of life (which for him was poetry and poetry alone) got disposed in its due and adequate multitudinous folds. We move with him but in images and references and vast and far correspondences; we eat but of strange compounds and drink but of rare distillations; and very soon, after a course of this, we feel ourselves, however much or however little to our own advantage we may on occasion pronounce it, in the world of Expression at any cost. That, essentially, *is* the world of poetry—which in the cases known to our experience where it seems to us to differ from Browning's world does so but through this latter's having been, by the vigour and violence, the bold familiarity, of his grasp and pull at it, moved several degrees nearer us, so to speak, than any other of the same general sort with which we are acquainted; so that, intellectually, we back away from it a little, back down before it, again and again, as we try to get off from a picture or a group or a view which is too much *upon* us and thereby out of focus. Browning is 'upon' us, straighter upon us always, somehow, than anyone else of his race; and we thus recoil, we push our chair back, from the table he so tremendously spreads, just to see a little better what is on it. This makes a relation with him that is difficult to express; as if he came up against us, each time, on the same side of the street and not on the other side, across the way, where we mostly see the poets elegantly walk, and where we greet them without danger of concussion. It is on this same side, as I call it, on *our* side, on the other hand, that I rather see our encounter with the novelists taking place; we being, as it were, more mixed with them, or they at least, by their desire and necessity, more mixed with us, and our brush of them, in their minor frenzy, a comparatively muffled encounter.

My critical prowess boggles at the specific questions raised by this brilliant generalized reaction. Because *The Ring and the Book* is a freak, a poem conceived in an essentially novelistic technique, one would prefer to start by considering the poetic novel rather than the novelistic poem. Novels are sometimes said by critics, more often by reviewers, to be 'poetic', though a fundamental contradition in terms is involved. The obligation is on the novelist, however singular or steadfast his narrating consciousness, to give a sense of multiplicity of viewpoints, of life as it is lived in a world of uninterrupted awareness, taking in the depths as well as the heights of human experience. No such obligation is on the poet. Nevertheless there is a real sense in which novels are poetic, far beyond the conventional response of a reviewer to an author's name, theme or style. The language of prose is figurative as is the language of poetry, and a novel may be dominated and unified by imagery. Moreover, at the centre of many novels, sometimes at the crucial scene or the crucial moment of the crucial scene, the novelist depends—not on some denseness of description or psychological insight—but on a likeness that is characteristic of poetry so as to bring home his purpose, to set reverberations echoing. It is easy for me to illustrate this from my own work and I ask indulgence for doing so, but the business has general application. I'll take just one example, the closing sentence of my novel *The Ruined Boys*. The book's theme is the complete change in a boy's view of life as a result of the events narrated, particularly his view of the morality of his school and of the character of the headmaster. Here is the sentence:

As in those drawings by Stubbs a horse is depicted in the verisimilitudinous action of trotting but the representation is actually of a horse's skeleton, so it seemed to Gerald that the school and the Headmaster, though going through the plausible motions of ordinary existence, were in fact demonstrating a truth about the nature of being which they possessed without knowing and which it had taken their death to reveal.

We may remark that in a poem the image of the Stubbs drawing could probably only have been introduced with some sense of strain. Its comparative prolixity and the necessity to indicate its various correspondences with the matter in hand would have caused an unacceptable awkwardness. In prose, the amplitude required passes un-noticed and, coming at the end of sixty or so thousand words, its allusive power is enhanced. And its use for the author in suggesting, among other things, that in his book he has been anatomizing a dead society gives the image a far from decorative function.

One might add here that the dual practitioner usually has a keen sense of what imagery is apt for poetry and what for prose fiction. It's not just, as may be inferred from what I've said already, that certain tropes don't lend themselves to verse's succinct and rhythmical nature, though that consideration enters into the calculation. There is also what may be called the sore thumb aspect: though poetry allows (indeed, often calls for) the striking aperçu, the imagery of a poem mustn't obtrude from its general texture. There is an amusing instance in a poem by Aldous Huxley: 'his unshaven face / Still like a record in a musical box.' The comparison strikes entertainingly home but we feel, particularly in the general context of Huxley's poetic style, that the image really belongs to a novel or short story.

I'm strongly convinced that prose fiction, indeed, is capable of admitting a wider range of imagery than poetry—for the reasons I've given and also because the life on the novelist's side of the street must reveal its squalor and triviality, its anxious or comic breathing, sweat and talk. The greater indulgence of the novel as to what imagery it will admit corresponds, of course, to the mode of its composition. The writing of a fictional narrative over a period of months, perhaps years, requires an almost day to day hook-up between the author's current life and subconscious, and his piling manuscript. No wonder the novel is the most intimate of forms. The writing of lyric poetry works almost the other way. The hook-up between life and work is by no means so continuous or prolonged. The poem's imagery is more a matter of selection than inclusion; more a matter of chance. The observations of the poem, the likenesses it discovers, are, compared with the novel, almost alarmingly sparse. And the poem, starting from its compelling donnée or image, usually makes its further discoveries, sustains its narration, finds its form, by a process of refinement rather than extension, a process of interior working, of technical difficulties avoided or overcome, a process more likely to throw up generalizations than observations, or at any rate conjunctions meaningful only in the poem's own terms. To return to Aldous Huxley, one sees now that his poetry has been collected for the first time, though it was written in the period from the middle of the First War to the end of the Twenties, that his attempt to enlarge poetry's subject matter lacked the depoeticization of poetry's diction which should have accompanied the attempt—so that, as in my previous illustration, what is novel and striking in the verse seems to belong more properly to prose.

In saying all this one's conscious that one has acceded to prose fiction's having permanently annexed the 'poetic' areas of life as well as those more mundane tracts which were initially its special preserves. I think this must be so. The novel very soon developed poetic qualities—thematic imagery, ambiguous characterization, symbolic narration, critical morality, and so forth—while continuing marvellously to extend its naturalistic powers: against such resources poetry cannot seriously compete in that field. *The Ring and the Book*, despite other attempts at the novel in verse, remains a freak.

It follows, I believe, that all efforts to call poetry over to the novelist's side of the street risk failure, none more so than the informality of language and metre, and the autobiographical detail, of much recent verse. The very technique of poetry puts the art at a distance, while the attempted truthfulness of the poetic 'I' is a restricted and pallid affair compared with the verisimilitude of which the novelist is capable, with his masks and narrative devices and control over space and time. One need only think of the character which John Berryman presents of himself in *Love and Fame* and then of Thomas Mann's imaginary composer in *Doctor Faustus*. Poets needn't be down-hearted about this. After all, it's the death of the novel that is always being confidently predicted.

Though no return may be possible to the poem comparable in length to the novel, and though the poet may have yielded to the novel complications of plot and character, this is not of course to say that in the foreseeable future only the lyric poem is viable or that the extended poem may not be written. Poets have something to learn, it seems to me, from the very break-up in the novel's form that to some critics has seemed to indicate its impending demise. One can envisage a new large poetic talent reviving the genre of W. H. Auden's *The Orators*, a work that in parts has similarities to the experimental novel—the abrupt changes of material, the intimate journal, the powerfully emotive but rag-bag air. My own feeling is that such stuff, in prose or not, preferably belongs to the poem rather than prose fiction, that prose fiction is well shot of it. The suspension of disbelief is harder to achieve in the novel than poetry and the process isn't helped by wilfulness of form. On the other hand, poetry seems to stand, even thrive on, outrageous imaginative collage, provided the poet remains in formal control. To adapt some words in Nietzsche's *The Birth of Tragedy*: in the novel Dionysus must speak in the language of Apollo; in poetry, in the last analysis, Apollo uses the tongue of Dionysus.

V

Fascinating Rhythm

Every schoolboy knows—or at any rate every undergraduate reading English knows—that the essay published in 1602 by Thomas Campion called *Observations in the Art of English Poesie* was a curiously reactionary production. Reactionary on two counts: it argued against rhyme in English poetry; and in analysing rhythm it used the classical system of long and short syllables. This reactionariness is all the more curious because Campion in his own verse not only used rhyme freely but is also one of the great masters of rhythm. Moreover, he was an outstanding musician and much of his verse was written to be set to music. With these things in mind it must strike us that there's something fishy about the bad reputation of Campion's essay. Surely such a fine practising poet couldn't have theorized about his art in a vacuum? Later I want to look at the essay and try to make sense of it from Campion's point of view and in the light of our own concept of English prosody.

There seems little doubt that rhythm, alas, is the root of the matter in poetry. One accompanies the remark with a sigh because so many other elements in poetry seem more interesting and because, after all, in the sophisticated state of the art in our time one feels somewhat infra dig in admitting, in concerning oneself with, the residual influence of the tom-tom or the capstan. Even the more complicated notion of the connection between the rhythms of poetry and of the human body, like breathing and heart-beats, lacks great appeal. In the chapter of Christopher Caudwell's *Illusion and Reality* which lists the characteristics of poetry, the statement 'Poetry is rhythmic' appears in pride of place, and as a Marxist Caudwell had no particular axe to grind on rhythm's behalf. And one's whole experience as a poet brings home to one that what prevents a poet from being a poet all the time—the business of inspiration—is not so much the lack of ideas or perceptions as the trickiness of casting them into rhythmical form.

Of course, if it were merely a matter of arranging one's aperçus in a pre-determined prosodic form, of obeying a set of rules, the matter would be largely one of ingenuity in which patience and a puzzle-solving skill would play the greatest part and there would be no need for such high falutin concepts as waiting for the descent of the Muse. Naturally, this kind of craft has its place, as in any art, but the rhythms required by the poet are not entirely the result of rules—indeed the rules are constantly being altered and enlarged by the poets' practice. I would want to adopt pretty well everything said by T. S. Eliot on these matters throughout his criticism. I think of a lecture he gave at Glasgow University in 1942, 'The Music of Poetry' (reprinted in *On Poetry and Poets*), when he said, following some remarks about prosodic rules: 'Whether poetry is accentual or syllabic, rhymed or rhymeless, formal or free, it cannot afford to lose its contact with the changing language of common intercourse.' Precisely: for the greatest block a poet can feel at the start of a poem is that his language is too literary, even slightly archaic, and this often comes from lighting on a rule-obeying or derived rhythm instead of a rule-making and personal rhythm. And in the very search for a conversational diction the poet is led into this difficult area of a less rigid or at any rate less hackneyed rhythm. In the phrase used on another occasion, in the early piece called 'Reflections on Vers Libre' (reprinted in *To Criticize the Critic*), the question is one of the 'constant evasion and recognition of regularity'.

I began with Thomas Campion because he outstandingly among
the excellent lyricists of the Elizabethan period possesses an individual rhythm, and one which seems closely connected with the
way his contemporaries spoke. One has only to glance down the
index of first lines in a collected Campion to find evidence of an
extraordinarily free and beautiful rhythmic talent: 'Are you what
your faire looks expresse?', for example, 'There is a Garden in her
face;' and 'Come away, bring thy golden theft'. On the mere
evidence of the first line it's sometimes hard to tell what the metre
of the poem is—for instance: 'Beauty, since you so much desire'.
Are there three beats in the line or four? If one accents the word
'so', as the sense might well require, the line, despite its eight

syllables, is quite plausibly three beat: 'Beauty, since you só much
desíre'. The following line of the poem, 'To know the place of
Cupid's fire', tells us that four beats are required, but to find them
is a problem. It would be absurd, for example, to conceive that
Campion had written three trochees and ended with an iambic
foot—'Beauty, since you so much desire'. All is explained when
one looks at the musical setting Campion made for the poem: the
time values of the notes indicate that the four emphases come on the
first syllable of 'Beauty', on 'you', on 'so' and on the second syllable
of 'desire'—'Beauty, since you so much desire'. This is a reading
that wrings the greatest sense out of the line and I suppose could
have been arrived at on that count alone.

The ambiguity of scansion of words for music may be seen in
crude form whenever words and music have a particularly close
association, as in old ballads where often words were made to fit
an existing tune. The process has continued in popular music.
For example, there is a remarkable line in the verse of the famous
duet in *Bitter Sweet*, Noël Coward's operette. The line is: 'All my
life I shall remember knowing you'. I suppose by admitting a
couple of trochees at the start it could be scanned as a wildly
irregular iambic pentameter—'All my life I shall remember

knowing you'. The line happens to have eleven syllables, but it seems unlikely that in the Twenties Sir Noël was experimenting with the eleven-syllable variation on the iambic pentameter I talked about in a previous lecture,* when discussing Marianne Moore's syllabics. Nor can one conceive that he had been studying Milton's practice, in *Paradise Lost*, of introducing an extra syllable into blank verse. As a matter of fact the musical setting proves that the line is intended to have four beats: there are four bars and the syllables with the longest note values are 'All', the last two syllables of 'remember', and 'you': 'All my life I shall remember knowing you'. I refuse to sing it. The duet from which the line comes is, of course, 'I'll see you again'—and one says 'I'll see you again' and not 'I'll see you again' because that is how Coward set the words, and not quite without point, either, since 'I' and 'see' and 'you' are pretty well of equal importance in the lyricist's mind (or heart)—and good syllables on which to throw the emphases of the waltz rhythm.

In his introduction to *The Lyrics of Noël Coward* the author is very modest about his knowledge of prosody, but it mustn't be supposed that he is incapable of vastly stricter metrical and stanzaic form—for example:

> *In tropical climes there are certain times of day*
> *When all the citizens retire*
> *To tear their clothes off and perspire.*
> *It's one of the rules that the greatest fools obey,*
> *Because the sun is much too sultry*
> *And one must avoid its ultry-violet ray.*

But Sir Noël himself explains, in the introduction I've referred to, why this kind of verse is less likely to result in the case of a

---

* See *Owls and Artificers*.

composer who is his own lyricist. The passage is so interesting and apropos of all that I've said so far that I'd like to quote it in full:

If a tune came first I would set words to it. If the words came first I would set them to music at the piano. This latter process almost invariably necessitated changing the verse to fit the tune. If you happen to be born with a built-in sense of rhythm, any verse you write is apt to fall into a set pattern and remain within its set pattern until it is completed. This is perfectly satisfactory from the point of view of reading or reciting, but when you attempt to set your pattern to a tune, either the tune gives in and allows itself to be inhibited by the rigidity of your original scansion or it rebels, refuses to be dominated and displays some ideas of its own, usually in the form of unequal lines and un-expected accents. This is why I very seldom write a lyric first and set it to music later. I think that the best lyrics I have written are those which have developed more or less at the same time as the music. All this of course inevitably makes the reading of lyrics more complicated than the reading of straight verse which was never intended to have a musical setting. Unless the reader happens to know the tune to which the lyric has been set, his eye is liable to be bewildered by what appears to be a complete departure from the written rhythm to which his ear has been subconsciously accustomed.

While I couldn't quarrel with Coward's practice and wouldn't want seriously to quarrel with his thesis (though he neglects the rebellion in English poetry against strict rhythms), I think his observations must call for a couple of warnings. The first is that the composer can do much more with an existing lyric than Coward is inclined to allow. Sullivan, for instance, doesn't seem to have felt much hampered by the metrical strictness of Gilbert's lyrics. Arthur Lawrence, in his biography of Sullivan, gives an account of a talk he had with the composer on this subject. Sullivan said that the first thing he had to decide on was the rhythm, and taking the lyric 'Were I thy bride' from *Yeoman of the Guard*, sat down and worked out eight different rhythmical versions in the form of dummy bars. 'My first aim,' Sullivan added, 'has always been to get as much originality as possible in the rhythm, approaching the question of melody afterwards. Of course, melody may come before rhythm with other composers, but it is not so with me. If I feel that I cannot get the accent right in any other way, I mark out the metre in dots and dashes, and it is only after I have decided the rhythm that I proceed to notation.'

My other warning about Sir Noël's observations is the perhaps obvious one that past a certain point of irregularity nothing can save the lyric from doggerel and in that state it can have no viable existence divorced from the music. This, even more than the reach-me-down statements in its content, is why the pop lyric often fails to survive on the page. Some young poets today have actually imitated this doggerel element in the pop lyric in poems not intended for music, and with disastrous results.

One asks oneself whether for both the sensitive composer and the good poet, the rhythm can ever make nonsense of the words. George Gershwin, who was not his own lyricist, often does the unexpected in the fitting of his music to words. But we usually feel, beyond his respect for the meaning of the lyric, that his music is discovering subtleties in the most commonplace of words. 'How long has this been going on?'—when he has to set that, a line of regular iambic tetrameter, surely he sees how banal it would be to emphasize the word 'this' as the underlying stress pattern of the
⏑　／　⏑　／　⏑　／　⏑　／
words requires: 'How long has this been going on?' What he does is to give the line three beats only—on 'long', the first syllable of 'going' and on 'on'. The three middle words, including the word 'this', are unaccented, giving the effect of a little skip in the middle
⏑　／　⏑　⏑　⏑　／　⏑　／
of the line—'How long has this been going on?' It is the action itself and the action's duration that Gershwin brings out, and how right it seems when he does it. Perhaps his brother Ira, who became almost exclusively his lyricist, grew deliberately to plant ambiguities of stress in his lyrics, less from carelessness about getting the metre strictly correct than from a wish to stimulate George's inspiration:

That certain feeling
The first time I met you.
I hit the ceiling.
I could not forget you.

There is an extra syllable in each of the second and fourth lines:
what is the composer to do about them? Gershwin's solution was
to make an anapaest of the words 'The first time', and give the
fourth line an extra beat.

I think a poet must envy the freedom of the composer in this
matter of stress. In Gershwin's song 'Fascinating rhythm' the lyric
to some extent prefigures the beat of the music, but it is difficult to
read the first line of the chorus (which is the title of the song) other

than as a three-beat line—'Fascinating rhythm'. Gershwin, of
course, makes it two-beat, with four short and unaccented notes in

the middle of the line—'Fascinating rhythm'—rendering the
rhythm truly fascinating and getting rid of the unsatisfactory and
ugly secondary stress in the word 'fascinating'.*

* I have left this passage about Gershwin as I originally prepared it since it was
derived from listening to the songs. It could have been supported (and slightly
modified) by the following passage from David Ewen's *A Journey to Greatness: The
Life and Music of George Gershwin,* which I came across later:

It is true that the melody usually came before the lyric. But it is also true — and
the fact must be emphasized — that Ira's song ideas, catchy titles, provocative
colloquialisms, ingenious verbal and rhythmic patterns were sparks which set
aflame the combustible fuel of George's musical imagination. A jingle-like effect
such as 'Do, do, do what you done, done, done before, baby' which Ira thought
up even before he wrote his lyric — lends itself so naturally to a mobile,
skipping melody that George was able to write this song for *Oh Kay* in a single
sitting, as soon as Ira presented him with the intriguing first line ... The song
'Sweet and Low Down' is one of several examples in which the lyricist pointed
the way for the composer. The digression in the chorus with the lines

Hear those shuffling feet
You can't keep your seat
Professor! start your beat
Come along get in it

demanded and received an unusual release in the melody which is one of the
high spots of that song.

'If God be for us who cán be against us?'—when Handel put that notorious wrong stress in a chorus of *Messiah* it was because of his imperfect knowledge of spoken English (though as has been pointed out to me it may be said that having decided on a 3/4 time rather than a 4/4 time he was rather stuck with that stress, and after all he didn't allow himself a great many days for *Messiah*'s composition). One has the feeling that many serious modern composers lapse in that way through recklessness, or indeed that they have a conviction that there should for interest's sake be a rebarbative opposition between their music's rhythm and the spoken rhythm of the texts they are setting; though possibly it's pitch rather than rhythm that's in question here—the apparently arbitrary ups and downs that in Peter Ustinov's parodies of Benjamin Britten are so hilariously characteristic. I may conveniently remark at this point what has probably been already painfully obvious, that my folly in lecturing on this baffling prosodic subject is heightened by my total ignorance of music's technical side.

Plainly, for most poets the sense of the words takes precedence over their rhythmical arrangement. Though a poet may have a wordless tune in his head, the words he eventually fits to it are usually determined by their meaning and the spoken rhythm of their syntax. In the case of some early poetry by Dylan Thomas one feels that the stanzaic form having been fixed, a good many of the lines are filled in simply with the juiciest iambs that came to mind. In the case of Swinburne there is an elaborate pre-determined pattern to which many of the other qualities of poetry must necessarily be sacrificed. But these are extreme and in many ways self-defeating cases. Poets do not possess the rhythmic freedom of the composer, nor can they take the prolix and irregular liberties of prose to tease out their meanings. They work—all too conscious

---

There is also an apposite passage in a letter from Gershwin dated March 8, 1934 to the librettist of *Porgy and Bess*, DuBose Heyward:

I would like to write the song that opens the 2nd Act, sung by Jake with the fish nets, but I don't know the rhythm you had in mind — especially for the answers of the chorus, so I would appreciate it if you would put dots and dashes over the lyric and send it to me.

of the paths nevertheless offered—in the area bounded by syntactical sense, conversational accents and the stress patterns of the medium.

Well, they so worked, at least, until recent times, when first poetry's stress patterns and then its syntactical sense began to be ignored. To touch on the poetry that waives syntactical sense would be outside my scope today, and in any case I don't think that particular kind of experimentation usually of any great general significance. The decline in the use of poetic stress patterns is another matter. It's interesting that in the table in *Illusion and Reality* which sketches 'The Movement of Bourgeois Poetry', Christopher Caudwell always uses the rhythmical changes in poetry to help distinguish poetry's various epochs which he regards, of course, primarily as socially determined. The rejection of rhythmic patterns by some poetry of the late bourgeois age he seems to see as part of the poet's rejection of the art's bourgeois past. Possibly Caudwell had in mind poets like Carl Sandberg and later, more left-wing poets who came out of the Whitman tradition. Caudwell also notes that where the social attitudes and content of poetry are in process of change, the question of form takes a second place. We must, in the Seventies, be less confident of briefly labelling these phenomena than was Caudwell in the Thirties. Besides, it's with the purely technical side of things I'm concerned here.

Poetry cannot ignore all patterns: to do so would condemn itself to prose. Much so-called free verse—particularly that of the past and that now written by mediocre poets—is verse of iambic metre, irregularly lineated. But the verse stemming from William Carlos Williams, so fashionable today, seems largely to be in sprung rhythm, with each 'foot' on a separate line or otherwise typographically notated. I say 'sprung rhythm' but the assembly of syllables constituting what I have called the foot may have more than one stress in it in the Gerard Manley Hopkins sense. The rationale of such verse is often given as the poet's individual voice or breath. Also, quite apart from such (as we may think) vague and arbitrary considerations, the typewriter or typographical notation of the poem is frequently opportunist in echoing the sense of the words—descending or ascending the page, for instance, if a staircase is mentioned—or isolating, for emphasis, some particular word or phrase.

Though the parameters of such verse may be thought rather crude, they are not altogether despicable. One's objections to them as the be-all and end-all of verse technique is the relative imprecision of type and blank paper to indicate some norm against which the syntactical emphases of the language are moving. Perhaps it isn't, after all, surprising that such verse is often read aloud by its authors in a traditional sing-song 'poetry' voice.

The question of hearing a poem is, of course, a vital one—all the way between the extremes of a public performance or in the mind's ear, direct from the page. One would find it hard to choose one's ideal reader aloud. The tune of a poem is more subtle than the tune usually put into it by an actor. If there is anyone worse than a mumbling poet it is an audibly rhetorical one. But the sound of a poem must be tested out and by sound I think I mainly mean rhythm: most English words make a satisfactory *noise* whether in poetry or not. And a most important part of the testing out is to appreciate the conflicts and accords of the poem's notional rhythm and its spoken rhythm. That is an additional argument for reading a poem aloud in a style that will make sense of it—reading for the meaning.

I think it isn't without interest to compare the performance of a poem with that of a piece of music. The reader of poetry has to make sense of it—but even that requirement is risked by certain eccentric actors, as anyone who ever heard Sir Frank Benson will testify. He should also be bound by the poem's rhythm. The executant musician has to prove his worth against—or, rather, in alliance with—a set of detailed instructions in every department of interpretation. Hans Keller has put the point beautifully (in an article called 'Is there performing genius?' in *The Listener* of 9 March 1972):

Even the great actor has a greater latitude [compared with the musical performer], a wider margin of error, in timbre, in pitch, and of course in time: not for him the all-important differences between a triplet rhythm and a dotted rhythm, or a dotted and a double-dotted rhythm, between a calculated *ritardando* or *meno mosso* and the spontaneous breath of living agogics—as Hugo Riemann called all fractional, unpremeditated, inspired rubatos ... Where there is no strict metre in the listener's mind, the performer can't deviate infinitesimally from it.

Though there isn't the opportunity in the reading of poetry for 'agogics' of that degree of subtlety, poetry's underlying rhythm does lay on its reader a performing obligation of similar order.

In a rather good book about modern poetry, *The Society of the Poem*, published in 1971, the author, Jonathan Raban, discussed the prosody of Philip Larkin's poem 'Mr Bleaney'. The poem is written in quatrains of iambic pentameter, rhyming *abab*. I just want to quote the first two and a half lines of the poem (the speaker is a landlady, showing a room to a prospective lodger):

> '*This was Mr Bleaney's room. He stayed*
> *The whole time he was at the Bodies, till*
> *They moved him.*'

The critic, Mr Raban, is alert to the prosodic movement of the poem and is particularly acute in pointing out the ironic contrast between the grave metre and stanza, and the banal lower middle-class properties of the poem. But he misses, it seems to me, the way Larkin uses metre here, as he often does, to point his meaning. For instance, Raban says that 'the opening two words of the poem make up, not an iambic, but a trochaic foot'. This can't be so. If one makes a trochaic foot out of 'This wás' there are two alternative consequences. One must go on making trochaic feet, a Hiawatha effect— 'Thís was Mr Bléaney's róom, he'. Which is absurd, since one is left with a single stressed syllable at the end of the line, 'stayed'— showing that one started, almost literally, on the wrong foot. The alternative is to make an anapaest out of 'Mr Bléa' so that the rest

of the line is iambic. But then the line has only four stresses instead
of five: 'This was Mr Bleaney's room. He stayed.' The answer, of
course, is that the opening word of the poem, 'This', constitutes a
foot by itself. The missing syllable in the foot we may imagine as
indicating the landlady throwing open the door of the room.
Moreover, since the landlady probably takes only one lodger and
in any case has just been discussing Mr Bleaney, it is apt that the first
syllable of the foot is missing—/Opens door/ 'This was Mr
Bleaney's room.'

Raban refers to 'a flurry of unaccented syllables' in the second
line: 'The whole time he was at the Bodies'. (The Bodies is presumably the familiar local way of referring to a company manu-
facturing car bodies.) One doesn't see this reading at all: it gets very
little sense out of the phrase. It may be conceived that the new
lodger is also an employee of 'the Bodies', in which case the phrase
would be read 'The whole time *he* was at the Bodies'—making
the line perfectly regular. But perhaps more likely is that the
previous discussion of Mr Bleaney laid emphasis on his prolonged
stay with the Bodies, so that the second foot of the line is intended
to be reversed—trochaic instead of iambic: 'The whole time he
was at the Bodies'. This reading also implies the landlady's hope
that the new lodger, too, will stay 'the whole time' his local
employment lasts.

Thomas Campion also constantly refers his meaning to his metre.
In isolation some of his lines look extremely odd—'Cold as thou
art, are thy loves that so much burnèd'. But this is the fifth line of a
poem in trochaic metre, so that when one gets to it one reads it
readily as 'Cold as thou art, are thy loves that so much burned', and
the sense comes with the accents. As Campion's latest editor,
Walter R. Davis, remarks, Campion 'accepts the iambic base of the
language'. But he is as restless as Pound or Auden under its domina-

tion. His is a remarkable anticipation of the revolt against the iambic line that has often taken place in English poetry, for the *Observations in the Art of English Poesie* may have been written as early as 1591. Yes, the nature of the language is iambic, but that is not the impression we receive from conversation. Poetry must have a metrical system, but such a system tends—unless it is going to be as madly elaborate as Swinburne's—to impose the monotony of the iambic. Hence (poets feel) we must turn to a system which permits escape from the iambic—a system of syllabics or typography or (in Campion's case) an ingenious mixture of metres. If one looks at the *Observations* one finds, for instance, that Campion's perhaps most celebrated lyric, 'Rose-cheekt Laura, come', is composed according to a strict recipe of mixed trochees and spondees. Part of its haunting music is due, I think, to the feeling one has that the iambic is constantly about to assert itself:

> *Rose-cheekt Laura, come,*
> *Sing thou smoothly with thy beawties*
> *Silent musick, either other*
> *Sweetely gracing.*

It was one of Samuel Daniel's damaging points in his reply to Campion (*A Defence of Rhyme Against a Pamphlet Entituled 'Observations in the Art of English Poesie'*) that the eight new metres for which Campion had given the recipes were really only artificial variations on the old iambic pentameter. Daniel has always had a pretty good press but here he is appealing rather outrageously to the English dislike of systems, innovations and foreign names. The fact is that few English poets have wanted or been able to exploit the kind of word-music suggested by Campion's forms. They may have felt they had bigger artistic fish to fry; and certainly the technical labour involved is great. Auden is one of the few English poets who springs to mind whose serious purposes would not be daunted by the severest of technical difficulties. Auden has in fact written poems where lines in one metre alternate with lines in another, and this is precisely one of the novelties prescribed by Campion's pamphlet.

Campion didn't, as Daniel's reply has made some people imagine, want to abolish rhyme — he said merely that it should be 'sparingly used'. That so essentially simple a device as rhyme is always in danger of becoming a 'tedious affectation' has struck many later poets. Perhaps it should almost always be campaigned against, like corporal punishment, but brought back in lax times.

In holding on to the notion of long and short syllables Campion gets into undesirable complications, but one senses that he is worried that the wholly stress view of English verse tends to lose syllables, as music never does. 'The numeration of syllables is not so much to be observed,' he says, 'as their waite and due proportion.' Once again there is an appeal to the speaking voice — or the singing voice, for, as Eliot has said, 'singing is another way of talking'. ('The Music of Poetry'.) On the other hand, Campion must surely have done some simple arithmetic with syllables, if only to make sure in his songs that the second and subsequent stanzas were going to fit the musical setting.

In down-grading the role of rhyme, in prescribing mixed metres, in trying to retain the differentiation between metres by augmenting the test of syllabic stress with the test of syllabic time, Campion wanted if not exactly to make the writing of verse more difficult at least to try to ensure that the intellectual skills of the craft would have to be cultivated. And he was writing, after all, at a time when the memory was vivid of poetry being in a sad state of metrical uncertainty, varying from doggerel to metrical jog-trot, with rhyme often acting as no more than a merely mechanical attempt to ensure that what was being written was not prose. (There are some interesting thoughts on considerations such as these in *Thomas Campion: Poet, Composer, Physician* by Edward Lowbury, Timothy Salter and Alison Young.)

As a practitioner, one's sense is that prosody mustn't make things *terribly* difficult. (I say 'prosody' — confining the thing to metre — because one would have to choose a very perverse stanza form to make rhyme daunting rather than a spur. Finding three rhymes, twice over, in the octave of a Petrarchan sonnet has never put poetasters off the form; and even sequences of rondels have been undertaken, a similar exercise but one of the rhyme sounds actually requiring four rhymes.) The regular alternation in the same poem of lines of varying metres is, as I've said, particularly hard to bring off and it's significant that some of Coleridge's metrical experiments were never fitted out with more than, so to speak, dummy words — they are just nonsense verses:

> *I wish on earth to sing*
> *Of Jove the bounteous store,*
> *That all the Earth may ring*
> *With Tale of Wrong no more.*
> *I fear no foe in field or tent,*
> *Tho' weak our cause yet strong his Grace:*
> *As Polar roamers clad in Fur,*
> *Unweeting whither we were bent*
> *We found as 'twere a native place.*

Nevertheless, without this kind of interest and such experiments, Coleridge wasn't likely to have hit on such fertile discoveries as the sprung rhythm of 'Christabel'.

I think poets, especially when the *zeitgeist* so much dictates which forms are thought right, are often too easily convinced that the metre (and the form) of a poem has arrived with its *donnée*. This must be so particularly in a time when *vers libre* of the blank-space-determined kind is so dominant. All ideas for poems, preliminary, jottings, notes thrown up in the course of writing, begin to look like poetry in themselves. What about the following? (I have added some punctuation and regularized upper and lower case.)

> *Where are you now? Is it true that you shed the*
> *sun-burn & became pale, white? Did you appear*
> *in the Post Office in 1916? Is it true that*
> *Pearse called on you by name of Cuchulain?*
> *Certainly we have need of you. The vague flood is at its*
> *height from one quarter alone; from all four quarters is coming.*
> *Come back with all your Pythagorean numbers!*

There are obvious repetitions and clumsiness there which any poet would want to clear up. But had the lines been written today (they are part of Yeats's first draft of 'The Statues') can we imagine them being transformed into anything like this?

> When Pearse summoned Cuchulain to his side,
> What stalked through the Post Office? What intellect,
> What calculation, number, measurement, replied?
> We Irish, born into that ancient sect
> But thrown upon this filthy modern tide
> And by its formless spawning fury wrecked,
> Climb to our proper dark, that we may trace
> The lineaments of a plummet-measured face.

The poet's work as interpreter of his life and age has always gone on alongside, as part of, his work as metrist — a truism which perhaps would only need to be uttered in a time of debased metrical standards.

Some of Robert Lowell's *Notebook* must surely strike us as draft material. Such material has its attractions, though mainly the umbrella on the operating-table kind of shock, and certainly such effect is not easy to recapture in the greater logic and polish of the finished poem. But to me the *Notebook* remains mostly foundations — which don't by any means reveal what may have been of grandeur in the design and which only here and there throw up a recognizable room or passage. 'My meter', Lowell said, in the 'Afterthought' to the book, 'fourteen line unrhymed blank verse sections, is fairly strict at first and elsewhere, but often corrupts in single lines to the freedom of prose. Even with this licence, I fear I have failed to avoid the themes and gigantism of the sonnet.' One sympathizes with his suspicion of the sonnet, but why, then, choose for the poem units of fourteen lines? And I feel sure that it's the metrics of the poem that so often gives the sense of a fine work aborted. So, too, I think one can already see that in such presently adulated work as Sylvia Plath's last poems the final force and effect is often sadly let down where the form is *ad hoc*.

If a collection like Lowell's *Notebook* may be felt to be short on metre's transforming and proportioning power, how far from finished must one regard the work of those who would think anything in the nature of metrical rules irrelevant to the writing of verse. Kingsley Amis once had the notion that the best advertising slogan for beer was 'Makes You Drunk'. The best advertisement to the poet for metre — and rhyme — might be 'Makes You Work', though the fundamental purpose is quite other.

The history of our language is complex. Also, it's always in a state of change, particularly in its conversational form. Poets are — or should be — rather more reliable than journalists or academics in preserving the standards of the language in work which is neither trendy nor archaic. Like Campion, one possibly exaggerates the need for classicism, and this is not only because the state of metrics is so uncertain but also because one doesn't see where, except in poetry, other qualities are possibly to be maintained. Besides, with Campion in mind we must think, too, of the marvellous rhythmic subtleties, approaching those of music, that formal metres can engender.

Professors and Gods

This year of 1972 is the centenary of Nietzsche's long essay, *The Birth of Tragedy*. For me the date came up when a magazine asked for a poem for a special number to mark the anniversary, the request arising because in an earlier poem contributed to the magazine I'd mentioned Nietzsche's relations with the Swiss historian Jacob Burckhardt. However, Nietzsche is not a writer I care for nor one I've widely explored. I can't read German and it seems clear that much of Nietzsche's flavour is lost in translation, despite his being a writer of ideas. It must be admitted that there is something heroic in an artist's willingness to undergo, to urge along, even the most rigorous historical trends of his times, but in Nietzsche's case and with our hindsight about the German and other militarism and violence of this century, I think the heroism is detestable even though we can't completely withhold admiration. In fine, my view is like that of Jeeves, who once remarked to Bertie Wooster: 'You would not enjoy Nietzsche, sir. He is fundamentally unsound.'

The Birth of Tragedy is a book of remarkable insights but it arouses the old ambivalent feelings about its author. Its central notion, the Apollonian and Dionysian principles in art, has become rather a commonplace of criticism, particularly in America, but it remains a suggestive approach. Apollo as the symbol of order, Dionysus as the symbol of unfettered inspiration — the temptation has been not only to view literature in these terms but also to use them to classify writers themselves. And when the symbols have seemed to become somewhat frayed, others have been invented, of similar opposition: for instance, palefaces and redskins. I don't know that such labelling of individual authors is more than a sophisticated parlour game, that very much has been done when one has put Emerson and Hawthorne among the palefaces and Whitman and Melville in the redskin camp. In *The Birth of Tragedy* Nietzsche uses his symbols with disturbing subtlety. For him, for example, 'the intricate relation of the Apollonian and Dionysian in tragedy must really be symbolized by a fraternal union of the two deities: Dionysus speaks the language of Apollo; Apollo, however, finally speaks the language of Dionysus.' Though Nietzsche is here dealing specifically with tragedy, I think we must feel that his remark applies to poetry in general, possibly all art.

This is a hard lesson for perhaps both paleface and redskin. Today, particularly among the young, there is a strong feeling that order in art, particularly syntactical and prosodic order in poetry, stifles much, even all, that is instinctive, original, life-enhancing, spontaneous and arousing in the creative impulse. It is a feeling that our new educational systems often encourage from the earliest age. It sometimes lies at the root of student rebelliousness about schools of art and university courses of study. But I don't want to labour the erroneousness of these views: it seems to me an evident truth that to enter in any serious way the temple of art the rules of him whom Nietzsche characterizes as the true father of the gods must be mastered. What is a much bitterer pill is for the Apollonian writer to acknowledge that in the last analysis the value of his work rests on the Dionysian principle.

Moreover, the pill has to be swallowed in the life outside art (if it can sensibly be said that life outside art exists for the artist).

After Nietzsche's collapse in the tertiary stage of syphilis he recovered consciousness and over a few days wrote and posted a number of extraordinary but mad letters, his last communications as a writer. One to Burckhardt, who had formerly been his elder colleague, began: 'In the end I would much rather be a Basel professor than God; but I have not dared push my private egoism so far as to desist for its sake from the creation of the world.' One sees what he meant. The strain of continuing to invent is one that perhaps a good few artists would like to be shot of. The testing of their ideas in the inimical world often contrasts unfavourably with a life of contemplation and study. The choice of Burckhardt as a symbol of the renunciation of creativity was a pregnant one, for though Burckhardt's own work and sensitivity to creation were remarkable, his stoicism was at the other pole to Nietzsche's joy about even atrocious times. Burckhardt had once written that he had been prepared, at every stage of his life, to exchange his existence for a never-having-been. That his fear and disillusion and pessimism had not in fact resulted in suicide is, in a way, heroic too, but the heroism is not that of the great artist. It might be said, I suppose, that the outlook of a fine poet like Thomas Hardy was not so different, but I feel that Hardy's stoicism stopped far short of sacrificing his experiences in life, however random and meaningless he might conceive them to be. And Nietzsche's desire to be Burckhardt (if we allow it to be unironic) was only a passing weakness: the same day of the Burckhardt letter he put at the end of a letter to another friend the signature 'Dionysus'!

For nearly two centuries Western literature has above all recognized, admired, encouraged the Dionysian principle. This comes out not only in the kind of literature created but also in many writers' feeling that creativity is not the end of their function — that the poem having been written the poet is under a further duty to play a part in the world of action. To play a part, that is to say, precisely because of his gifts and responsibilities as a poet. The situation has often contained elements of the farcical, even when resolving itself in a tragic way. Byron in Greece is a

familiar example. Norman Mailer and Robert Lowell advancing
on the Capitol is a modern instance. My own youth, in the
decade leading up to the outbreak of the Second World War,
was steeped in the indecisions and frustrations arising from the
sense that mere writing was inadequate for the situation, yet
politics was an activity for which the poet was constitutionally
unfitted.

> *Wandering between two worlds, one dead,*
> *The other powerless to be born*

— Matthew Arnold's feeling, expressed in the mid-nineteenth
century, was shared by many poets of the nineteen-thirties, and the
malaise was no easier to bear because they believed they knew
more precisely how the new world was to be brought into being.
Nor did it help much in a practical way to be able to characterize
oneself as part of the bourgeoisie, and to know that the
bourgeois life precluded the kind of complete commitment
sought. In fact, one wasn't slow to criticize those (among whom
Stephen Spender put the point most clearly) who believed that
there could be value in writing frankly out of the weakness of
the self-conscious bourgeois position.

Age has enured one to the ambiguous role, even made it seem
defensible. In the realm of commitment, too, Dionysus speaks the
language of Apollo. I don't think it's quite a case of ratting on
youthful beliefs and endeavours; rather that one comes to see
that in art there must be a distancing effect even in the matter of
one's strongest and most urgent feelings and beliefs. I mean that
literary expression for the most part precludes the directly factual,
the directly emotional: it must employ instead the equivalent
figure and the more formal tone.

> *I met Murder on the way* —
> *He had a mask like Castlereagh* —

Even such a straightforward and vehement beginning (the

standard of which, moreover, Shelley could not keep up for long)
depends on the reversed simile, and the tone is basically ironic.
The theme of an interesting recent book called *Imagination and
Power* by Thomas R. Edwards was that when a poet is driven to
write about 'public men' and 'public conditions' his imagination
becomes much more like that of other men — he is 'led to something like a provisional and partial identification with ordinary
men and their outlook'. However, it is the other and more
important part of Professor Edwards's thesis that though such
poetry implies a broadening of the poet's scope, if it is to be
successful it must retain a critical power towards the men and
conditions it treats, thus clearing away the fog of rhetoric and
received feelings that surround them.

Though one may admit the rationale of his thesis, I think one
is uneasy about the author's assumption that the division of men
into poets and non-poets has some special significance. It's true
that at certain times (the Nineties, say) and in certain places
(Cwmdonkin Drive, Swansea) some poets have thought of themselves as privileged and set apart, but what poets and non-poets
share is overwhelmingly more massive than what separates them.
It's no doubt the case that a successful 'public' poem will have a
kind of truth that will spotlight and complicate figures and issues
that often conspicuously seem, treated elsewhere, to lack truth.
But the poet is embedded like other men in his class and times,
and his struggle there matters, as well as his struggle with poetic
words and ideas. He, too, is at the mercy of simple misjudge-
ments and received ideas. Professor Edwards quotes the end of
one of the poems in Robert Lowell's *Notebook* on Robert
Kennedy:

> *Doom was woven in your nerves, your shirt,*
> *woven in the great clan; they too were loyal,*
> *and you too were loyal to them, to death.*
> *For them like a prince, you daily left your tower*
> *to walk through dirt in your best cloth. Untouched,*
> *alone in my Plutarchan bubble, I miss*

you, you out of Plutarch, made by hand —
forever approaching our maturity.

(I give the slightly revised version in the English edition of
Notebook.) Professor Edwards's commentary on the passage rightly
draws attention to 'the way the poet in his "Plutarchan bubble",
securely remote from the politician and his dreadful end, is made
aware of a significance that threatens to render irrelevant his own
role as contemplative man and the values that support that role'.
But about the crucial final line — Robert Kennedy 'forever
approaching our maturity' — Edwards's view is that the poem
makes us 'recognize that "our maturity" is in a way feeble and
pitiful compared to the princely potentiality [the dead politician]
will now eternally represent'. Certainly Lowell is ironic in the
poem about the creative artist's way of life (it begins, in a passage
I haven't quoted, with images of loneliness, of a non-creative
period) but I don't think he is at all playing down the values held
by the creative artist, the values that Kennedy, not only in the
legend his life and assassination made but also in his unceasing self-
education, did grow nearer to. And the poem surely can't be
criticized on this score. Where it does cause misgiving, however,
is its acceptance of Kennedy in non-poetic terms. The depiction of
the Kennedy family as 'the great clan' and the omission of Robert
Kennedy's ambivalence, not to say shiftiness, about the political
issues that confronted him (not adequately subsumed in the
participle 'approaching'), make us feel that the poem's high terms
are unjustified.

   All poetry, even the poetry of commitment (perhaps particularly
that), must earn the values it intends to subsist by. And it must
earn them in the only way that poetry knows — through the
quality of its work; of its words, images, metrics, rhyme.
Rhetoric will never do by itself. I realize that we are in a difficult
critical area here: one can be seduced or put off by poetry's prose
ideas. All the same, one feels that in the working out of a good poem
the ideas that the fabric of the poem will not support drop out or
get modified. In another poem discussed by Professor Edwards,

the familiar 'Easter 1916', Yeats unerringly establishes the character of his dead heroes within the poem and relies only on a personal reaction, which would have been the same even had the poem been not in the least committed:

> This other man I had dreamed
> A drunken, vainglorious lout.
> He had done most bitter wrong
> To some who are near my heart,
> Yet I number him in the song;
> He, too, has resigned his part
> In the casual comedy;
> He, too, has been changed in his turn,
> Transformed utterly.

We mustn't forget, either, the part played by the verse form in this poem: the sprung-rhythm trimeters, rhyming and half-rhyming with some complexity; the handling of the tricky refrain. The work-load assumed by Yeats here, its successful outcome, as I've said, militating against any received response, is in some contrast to Lowell's rather casual and very variable blank verse.

I think in the Thirties some of us were possessed too much of poetry's importance and too little of its necessary impersonality. I mean, as to its importance, that our final aim was that our words should, in Yeats's phrase, send men out to be shot. With the pacifist poetry of 1917 and 1918 very much in our heads, we thought that in those times of equal crisis poetry ought again to try to influence action. With this sense went a desire for a larger audience. It was a desire that remained unfulfilled, despite some quite extraordinary efforts in the way of poetic drama, readings at political meetings and the appearance of verse in periodicals that circulated among the politically-conscious working-class. One sees today among the young a renewal of the notion of poetry's importance in a similar sense, and the notion is happily not confined to those who write the stuff. If I may try to bring out my own experience here I would say that poetry is important only so far as it exists not, on the one hand, for its own sake, nor, on the other, for the sake of its ideas and emotions. I've written elsewhere, in connection with the vast English Literature industry (particularly in the United States), that one has become aware of a somewhat excessive prestige attaching to poetry, coupled with a sense of guilt that one's own contributions have *ipso facto* acquired the honoured status. 'Observations on poetry and its enemies' was the sub-title of a recent critical book and, thinking in a jaundiced moment of the enormous amount of verse produced and the wilder claims for its effect by more romantic practitioners, my reaction was: Hurray for the enemies.

Poetry as our culture knows it (and, it seems to me, as any subsequent culture would know it which had inherited our civilized gains) is, in the word Freud applied to dreams, over-determined. The properties of the poem (including its language) may be used in several different ways in its interpretation. I think it was Christopher Caudwell who first applied the analogy, but everyone reading Freud's *Interpretation of Dreams* must have been struck with the amount of personal and social history, the symbolism and play on words, that lie behind the simplest dream. The box in the dream is not only the obvious female symbol: it is the very box we used to keep our toys in; the gift (in the Christmas box sense) we hope to receive; the name of the shop-keeper we visited on the day of the dream; and so forth. Of course, in poetry what lies behind must be made manifest in the poem itself — with this exception, however: the poet will assume in his reader a shared cultural history. As behind the dream there exists an enormous private world, so a lengthy cultural past subtends from every poem.

Such a past, as well as the echoes and homophones and the very syntax of the language, as well as the aptness of one object to stand, in the human mind, for another, makes for poetry's over-determination. All these may be considered to be the gifts of Dionysus, but they can scarcely be used unless the tools of Apollo — the progressive discourse of inner logic, the rhythmical form — have been at work to announce the artifact as a poem; indeed, to provide a milieu, as different from prose as the dream from waking life, where over-determinism can flourish. Apollo it is who makes 'box' the rhyme word and very often, too, gives it its pregnant qualifying adjective and its likeness to a quite disparate object.

'I think that great art is necessarily impersonal,' Dr Leavis said not long ago (the *Listener,* 16 December 1971). He was reviewing a book called *Xenia* by the Italian poet Eugenio Montale, and he began by recalling a meeting with Montale where the two of them quoted at each other Paul Valéry's *Le Cimetière Marin.* Leavis associated Eliot's espousal of a theory of impersonality with the American poet's admiration for Valéry, but Leavis's view was that Valéry's celebrated poem was a brilliant demonstration of the poetic art conceived as a game, a conception as foreign to Eliot's own poetry as it is to Montale's. In a lecture called 'From Poe to Valéry' (printed in *To Criticize the Critic*) Eliot recommended the exploration of a way of poetry written to the Valéry recipe: that is, that 'a poem should have nothing in view but itself' (Baudelaire's phrase) and 'that the composition of a poem should be as conscious and deliberate as possible, that a poet should observe himself in the act of composition.' I'm sure that modern poetry has paid too much attention to this recipe or to recipes very like it. Paradoxically enough, the poetry that has resulted, in the English-speaking world at any rate, has not been a calculated formality but a concentration in the poem on the poet's character and predicament as a poet.

I don't think it's far-fetched to see the solipsistic poem and the calculated poem as two sides of the same coin. The poem for its own sake is paralleled by the poet's existence for the sake of the poem. The poetry at the farthest remove from this would be Leavis's 'impersonal art'. Again there is a paradox, which Leavis explains when discussing *Xenia*:

> For a major poet such as Montale is, poetry is one's profoundest response to experience. The theme of *Xenia* is as central, important and moving as any human theme can be, and the reticence it requires of the poet is not a refusal to recognize the

full nature of what, intimately for him as sufferer, it in reality portends; but the contrary. It is the use of intelligence (and that involves the discriminations of sensibility — *l'intelligence*, I tell my students, is not the same as 'intelligence') that determines how the actual pondered sense of irrevocable loss can be defined and communicated — two verbs that mean one thing to the poet. 'Life' is a necessary word, but life is concretely 'there' only in individual lives, and Montale's art, so different from Eliot's as well as from Valéry's, achieves, devoted as it is to rendering with delicacy and precision his intensely personal experience, a profound and moving impersonality in the only way in which such impersonality *can* be achieved.

The bilingual edition of *Xenia* which Dr Leavis was discussing contained a foreword by the translator, Professor Singh, which compared Montale's work with the group of poems Thomas Hardy wrote after the death of his first wife. Those poems (and I think of them as including all the pieces Hardy wrote on the theme, not merely the ones under the heading 'Poems of 1912–13' in *Satires of Circumstance*) are outstanding in Hardy's work for the quality of personal emotion revealed. Yet they are far from what today would be labelled 'confessional' poetry. They have the impersonality of great art. Hardy's craftsmanship has much to do with this: his restless experimenting with stanza-forms and metres here pays off in a marvellous way — and indeed every poet must know, if only subconsciously, that a fitting subject-matter may only two or three times in his life-time match up with his technical labours. But intense feeling and craft are not the end of the story: the sequence brings to life the dead wife. The decline of the marriage and her unexpected death are shown not merely as the poet's tragedy but also hers.

It was your way, my dear,
To vanish without a word
When callers, friends or kin
Had left, and I hastened in
To rejoin you, as I inferred.

And when you'd a mind to career
Off anywhere — say to town —
You were all on a sudden gone
Before I had thought thereon,
Or noticed your trunks were down.

So, now that you disappear
For ever in that swift style,
Your meaning seems to me
Just as it used to be:
'Good-bye is not worth while!'

Even in such a slight poem the touches are those of a novelist —
and not because Hardy *was* a novelist but because the truth of the
situation required delineation of the third party herself as well as
the poet's emotion. Poetry in our time has lost much to the novel
(I fear inevitably so, though sometimes poetry can make do without the things lost) but it need not give up entirely what the novel
forces on the novelist, a viewpoint not always his own and a regard
for the situation of others. Moreover, in his encompassing of such
things the novelist usually finds that irony is an essential vehicle.
It's no accident that Dr Leavis remarks about the Montale poem
that 'wit, irony and humour . . . intensify the effect of profound
seriousness'.

In one of his *Music of Time* novels, Anthony Powell wrote that
'all classes of this island converse in understatement and irony'.
Apropos of that I have made the point elsewhere how curious it is,
therefore, that writers like Swift and Pope (and Mr Powell himself) often have to go on bearing misapprehension. Perhaps from
all literature, particularly poetry, the general expectation is for the
plainly Dionysian; and when it comes in Apollonian form as it so
often should, the expectation is disappointed. 'The Fur that warms
a king once warmed a bear' and 'Where slumber Abbots purple as
their wines' — such lines, by no means infrequent, make one
wonder how Matthew Arnold read Pope to pronounce him a prose
classic. For the effects here are by no means exhausted when the
wit and aptness of the figures are given their full consideration.

And (amplifying a notion I expressed in a previous lecture) even in prose, which will admit an imagery altogether more elaborate and more circumstantially specific than poetry, we may find Dionysian undertones taking a hand — if not in technical expression (since prose imitates poetry at its deadly peril, as Dickens's purple blank-verse passages show) then in obvious excitement of inspiration. Mr Powell's fiction, for example, is full of tropes. Widmerpool's hands, as a boy, 'were small and gnarled, with nails short and cracked, as if he spent his spare time digging with them deep down into the soil'. And in the same first volume of *The Music of Time* sequence, the housemaster's habit of putting his body into unusual postures is said to have given 'him the air of belonging to some highly conventionalized form of graphic art: an oriental god, or knave of playing cards'. Such things are thrown off merely as integral to the author's prose discourse. But occasionally an excitement grips Mr Powell and not only at the prospect of having to depict some climactic scene or dénouement of relationship. Here, for instance, is Dionysus at work when Captain Bithell is discovered in a drunken sleep:

He lay under the grey-brown blankets in a suit of yellow pyjamas, filthy and faded, knees raised to his chin. His body in this position looked like a corpse exhumed intact from some primitive burial ground for display in the showcase of a museum. Except that he was snoring savagely, cheeks puffing in and out, the colour of his face, too, suggested death. Watch, cigar-case, sleeping pills, stood on the broken chair beside the bed. In addition to these objects was another exhibit, something of peculiar horror. At first I could not imagine what this might be. It seemed either an ornament or a mechanical contrivance of complicated design. I looked closer. Was it apparatus or artefact? Then the truth was suddenly made plain. Before going to sleep, Bithell had placed his false teeth in the ashtray. He had removed the set from his mouth bodily, the jaws still clenched on the stub of the cigar. The effect created by this synthesis was extraordinary, macabre, surrealist. Again one thought of an excavated tomb, the fascination aroused in archaeologists of a thousand years hence at finding these fossilized vestiges beside Bithell's hunched skeleton; the speculations aroused as to the cultural significance of such related objects.

Though there were in the realms of poetry the corresponding examples of Eliot and Yeats, in the Thirties few would have prognosticated that an English realistic novel, depicting our times with unrivalled truth and detail, would have come from a novelist of the right. Mr Powell's offer, in all departments of his endeavour, to make his readers laugh has resulted, in *The Music of Time* sequence, in there being few areas of illusion about history or human conduct — the kind of journalistic illusion, for example, seen about Robert Kennedy in the Lowell poem. It's often said that Mr Powell writes from a High Tory point of view but I'm not sure we're ever really conscious of this. To take an obvious example, in *The Military Philosophers* when the narrator is in the Netherlands with his group of foreign attachés and they are taken to meet the Field Marshal (unnamed, though obviously Montgomery), nothing in the scene relies on any received or theoretical view of the British military leader or his role in the liberation of Europe from the Nazi régime. The scene itself is brilliantly observed, a good deal of its force coming out of the narrator's eye for social detail. Afterwards the narrator reflects on what he has seen:

The eyes were deepset and icy cold. You thought at once of an animal, though a creature not at all in the stylized manner of the two colonels at my Divisional Headquarters, reminiscent respectively of the dog-faced and bird-faced Egyptian deities. No such artificial formality shaped these features, and to say, for example, they resembled those of a fox or ferret would be to imply a disparagement not at all sought. Did the features, in fact suggest some mythical beast, say one of those encountered in *Alice in Wonderland,* full of awkward questions and down-right statements? This sense, that here was perhaps a personage from an imaginary world, was oddly sustained by the voice. It was essentially an army voice, but precise, controlled, almost

mincing, when not uttering some awful warning . . . There was
a faint and faraway reminder of the clergy, too; parsonic, yet
not in the least numinous, the tone of the incumbent ruthlessly
dedicated to his parish, rather than the hierophant celebrating
divine mysteries. At the same time, one guessed this parish
priest regarded himself as in a high class of hierophancy too,
whatever others might think.

The successive comparisons in this passage (as throughout *The
Music of Time*) refining and refining the apprehension in the
interests of truth, ensure a freedom and range of comment that
transcend the merely ideological.

Perhaps committed writing, particularly poetry, is constantly
seeking to be tragic. In his preface to *The Birth of Tragedy*
Nietzsche asks why the Greeks were in need of tragedy — 'a race
of men, well-fashioned, beautiful, envied, life-inspiring' in need
of 'the art-work of pessimism'? He answers himself with further,
yes-requiring, questions:

> Is pessimism *necessarily* the sign of decline, of decay, of failure,
> of exhausted and weakened instincts? . . . Is there a pessimism
> of *strength*? An intellectual predilection for what is hard, awful,
> evil, problematical in existence, owing to well-being, to
> exuberant health, to *fullness* of existence?

One sees only too clearly the attractiveness of assent here. Some
writers of our time, among them the greatest, such as Pound and
Yeats, have gone part way along that path, envisaging through
support of superficially heroic political movements the chance to
make, once again, high tragic art. One sees, too, in Nietzsche's
words the seeds of a bogus tragic art, fascist art, paralleled by the
will to ruin of a Hitler. What Nietzsche left out of account and
what the truly historically conscious modern artist must surely
realize, has been recently brilliantly encapsulated by Iris Murdoch
(in an address to the American Academy of Arts and Letters,
partly printed in the *New York Review of Books*, 15 June, 1972):

> All good tragedy is anti-tragedy. *King Lear*. Lear wants to enact

the false tragic, the solemn, the complete. Shakespeare forces him to enact the true tragic, the absurd, the incomplete.

Our attempts at tragedy in the Western world take place in an ambience largely of subjective values. Committed writing has often come to equal confessional writing. The absurdities of bodily existence; derangement through intoxication or psychic mal-adjustment; the blows of a largely self-inflicted fate — such ingredients of much presently-admired poetry depend for their effect on the presentation of a suffering individual. The world-view implied is nihilistic. It seems to me significant that where genuinely tragic elements in literature undoubtedly exist today, in the work of certain dissident Soviet writers, the basic attitude remains a belief in social man and in the continuity of tradition, the tragedy being man's fall from virtue and history's wrong turns. I was struck with the following pregnant passage in a book called *Nihilism* published not long ago by an American academic, Stanley Rosen:

> What we now call 'values' are first given by nature; second they are given by history; third they are dissolved or reduced to pure subjectivity. This is a one sentence history of the development of Nihilism in the modern European world.

We tend to regard it as merely eccentric of Yeats to have excluded the poetry of the First World War from his *Oxford Book of Modern Verse* on the ground that 'passive suffering is not a theme for poetry', particularly as one of the poets thus excluded was Wilfred Owen, who now seems among the most considerable of the century. Yet we must see behind Yeats's remark a sure instinct for poetry's possibilities and heights; a recognition of the necessity in tragedy for action and conflict. The point is that Owen's was not a poetry of passive suffering: in the context of 1917 and 1918 his pacifism was profoundly rebellious; also, his verse has more than a hint of a world view that sees the First War as the opening phase of an anti-human historical development.

I appealed earlier to the novel as a literary form diverting the author's attention from himself, but of course the novel, too, has in our age often succumbed to subjectivism. It's not merely (or perhaps at all) a question of first person narration or a single narrating consciousness; rather the complete reference of judgement to personal emotion. Moreover, in the field of the novel as in that of poetry, the art-work is often referred and considered in relation to the life of the author. The evaluation of Sylvia Plath as a poet now seems to her public quite inextricably bound up with her personal life and self-inflicted death; and so, too, the reputation of Norman Mailer as a novelist is based to a large degree on his public and private personae — how could his fiction by itself bear the amount of attention given to it by even serious critics?

In thinking of such extreme and on the whole degenerate romanticism I was reminded of a book published in the Twenties by the French critic Julien Benda, called *Belphégor*. The pieces it contained were for the most part actually written before 1914 but many of its principles could be restated today and illustrated from contemporary literature. In looking again at *Belphégor* it didn't surprise me to find the name of Nietzsche associated with the modern craze for subjective art and the penetration of the art-work by the author's life. Benda was saying, almost before I was born, that the subjective aesthetic was so engrained that his contemporaries, particularly young people, didn't even imagine that there could be any other. And he accounts for what even then he was prompted to call 'the cult of the theatre' by explaining that that 'form of art presents human emotion by the direct method; it seems to show us life itself, and allows us more effectively than any other art to forget the mind through which we are looking at it.'

One would add that today, probably more than ever, the theatre stands for the success of the second-rate and that the literary reputations it has made are often grotesquely over-valued. Comparative illiteracy is not necessarily a bar to success in the theatre. The actor, designer and producer may add interest or some verisimilitude to a deficient text. Moreover, the existence of television, not only as a vehicle for adapted stage plays but also as a repository for plays that have failed to make the stage, is a great encouragement to a mass of mediocre writers to pursue careers in the drama.

The author of *Belphégor* wasn't free from a certain facile snobbism when he gave as one of the reasons for the lowered standard of culture as:

> the entrance into French society of people of a different class, whose minds are in a state of nature (parvenus of trade, industry and finance, etc). It seems to us that generally speaking these sociological changes are not given their due importance in accounting for the decadence of the taste of society. We must realize that it is not simply that a class is changing its standards of value, but that because of political developments new arrivals, lacking culture, become members of that class, bringing with them their own standards of value . . . Just as it could be said that the triumph of Christianity is the substitution of the morality of the slave for that of the master, so the triumph of romanticism is the substitution in good society of the aesthetic of the savage for that of civilized man.

Serious questions are begged here, but we must be reminded of the lack of attention given in the criticism of contemporary art to the factor of the influx into the ranks of its creators of the half-educated. And I don't mean here merely pop art, in all its manifestations. In the graphic and sculptural arts, in aleatory music, in free verse, success is open to the amateur. The failing in our culture to renew itself is perhaps seen at its most disastrous when the classically-trained musical executant devotes himself to some footling, percussive and fiendishly difficult modern composition. For greater educational opportunity and deeper musicological research reacting on taste has resulted in a marvellous range of contemporary executants who, however, have not at all been matched by creative counterparts.

The failure of nerve of the cultured is extreme. I wish I'd time to quote more extensively from a recent article on a 'drop-out school' (her own term) by the American poet, Adrienne Rich (*New York Review of Books*, 15 June 1972). Much of it consists of an imaginary conversation between Miss Rich, as the parent of children at the school, and a sceptical interlocutor. The squalor of the school is made explicit: the insecurity and waywardness of its pupils is left more to the imagination. But I take a passage concerning science as illustration of the point about the continuance of culture I want to make. 'Do they study math (sic) and science?' asks the interlocutor. 'There was a math class but I gather it's recently turned into an oceanography class. We haven't yet had enough money for scientific equipment, though I believe if a student came in wanting to study, say chemistry, a way would be found.' The point is then put that no students will have a background to enable them to specialize in science nor even to find out whether science might interest them. Miss Rich replies:

It's hard to avoid hearing about science, if you're awake and alive in New York City. I do think that for a lot of kids, math represents the paradigm of the kind of exam passing, test taking pressure that has been so destructive to them in other schools. Also of the value-free, neutral, abstract kind of science which many young people in colleges, also are rejecting now.

Marcuse has put forward the not uncomic notion of 'repressive desublimation', seeing something calculated in the way bourgeois society turns a blind eye to pornography and permissiveness — the sexual satisfaction thus resulting having the effect of reducing political dissidence by the removal of drives deriving from sublimation. There is a parallel in what may be called 'repressive barbarianization' — the way bourgeois society diverts its potential rebels from acquiring the knowledge and techniques to enable them to gain effective positions from which to change that society. (It is among the children of the most cultured that repressive barbarianization especially flourishes!) And such diversion of the young by no means occurs merely in 'drop-out schools'. Tin Pan Alley has long been seen not only as a source of cash profits but also as an instrument inducing mindless conformity. Who would have thought education could paradoxically come to be regarded as a similar instrument?

I can't resist returning to *Belphégor* and quoting from its concluding paragraphs:

> With the future of social life and culture as we see it, we might even wonder whether this type of brain, artistic and at the same time intellectual, will ever make its appearance again; whether there will not always be the two types, forever incompatible and glaring furiously at each other — on the one hand the savant, completely unsecular, and on the other the layman, firmly opposed to all discipline of the intelligence; whether the synthesis, in one man, of the scientific mind of the Italian renaissance, and the artistic mind of Greece, that blaze of glory which was kindled in our seventeenth century literature . . . has not been forever extinguished in our time. . . . We see before us the day when good French society will repudiate even the slight support they now accord to ideas and organization in art, when their only enthusiasm will be for the actor's gestures or the impressions of women and children, the thunderings of lyric poetry and the ecstatic ravings of the fanatic.

It's not really uncanny that this accurate depiction (allowing for the Gallic rhetoric) of our woes was written sixty years ago. The operant forces have not changed. You'll have noticed that Benda also used the opposition with which I began — the savant and the layman, the professor and the god, paleface and redskin, Apollo and Dionysus. Truly civilized man has to play both roles but, as Benda asseverates, in the one person. And art should be a reflection of that tricky unity — a unity not of opposites but of the potentials in human nature and human society.

VII

English Poetry of the Two World Wars

For convenience I shall restrict 'war poetry' to the category of that written by poets who served in the armed forces. A critic must always welcome some limiting factor in his attempt at a comprehensive statement, and in this case one certainly wants to avoid having to try to sum up the whole poetry of the two periods in question. Moreover, the actual output of service poets tends to be manageably small. Wasn't it George IV who liked to hear of a writer's death because he knew then that he had the fellow complete on his shelves? There spoke a true critic.

Since, in both wars, the service poets who were any good were so few critics have tended to arrange them in a hierarchy of value, like a sporting league table or objects one might take on a desert island. I shan't myself be guiltless of this, but my reasons for preferring one poet to another I hope will have more than a competitive or arguable point. Indeed, I think it vital to get this question approximately right.

I also think that the category of service poets has a significance beyond the lecturer's or examiner's or anthologist's convenience. If one believes, with Thomas Mann, that 'in our time the destiny of man presents its meaning in political terms' the entry of the poet into the armed forces brings him inescapably face to face with that destiny. 'War is politics continued by other means' — we don't need Clausewitz's well-worn maxim to tell us that the soldier, sailor or airman is engaged in political activity. For the middle-class poet this will usually be a novel experience, to say the least. To be a political instrument, closely associated with masses of men, directly involved in events vital to his nation, to humankind — this is an experience that will test to the uttermost his powers as a poet, his powers of reflecting and interpreting experience. I say nothing of the preposterous terms of cruelty, violence and pain in which the activity is conducted.

Further, 1914, the date that starts the first of the two periods we have to consider, is a date of more significance than the preliminary graving on war memorials. The Marxist sees the year as the start of the general crisis of capitalism, but no special ideological beliefs are required to recognize it as a terrible dividing line, after which the continuity of world civilization was by no means guaranteed.

When Wilfred Owen's *Collected Letters* were published in 1967, one thing they showed with remarkable vividness was the crucial nature of the First War, and of active service, for the middle-class poet. The pre-war letters depict in great, often tedious detail the genteel poverty, the provincialism, the cultural desolation of the lower end of the English middle-classes in the days before 1914. Behind it all, Owen has resolved to be a poet. 'I seem without a footing on life,' he says, 'but I have one.' However, we can't help speculating on the stylistic and ideological dangers that might well have made his ambition impossible of decent fulfilment, had active service in the war not brought him up against the sharpest issues of the age. Until quite late in his short life his adulation of Keats, his admiration for dubious contemporary poets, the marginal aimlessness of his everyday occupation make us wonder how the story is going to come out right in the few pages remaining, how he is going to transform himself into — what one must call him, despite his early death, his truncated output — a major poet. Naturally, in no poet should the factor of native brain-power and ability be underestimated, but it is ideological truth which distances the poetry of Owen and of Siegfried Sassoon from such talents as Rupert Brooke and Julian Grenfell.

Of course, the best poetry of the First War was written towards the end of 1916 and in 1917 and 1918 when the patriotic and heroic illusions of those experiencing the war at first-hand had disappeared. It pre-figures and echoes the mood of the European peoples. Its pacifist content corresponds to the slogan of 'peace' of the revolutionary parties to which much of Europe eventually responded. The values it asserts, its confident con-demnation of suffering, military authority, profiteers, the indifferent and the deceived on the home front are, without being overtly political, as revelatory and astonishing as the analyses made by those socialist parties which had not thrown in their lot with the warring nationalist states. This poetry is remarkably at one with man's vital interests and aspirations at its historical moment of appearance, and that is a great source of its power and enduring interest.

As we move farther and farther away in time from the First War, so the critics' approach to its poetry becomes more and more sophisticated. It is essential, of course, for each epoch to revalue the poetry of the past, and one expects that with the passage of the years by and large a truer view will emerge. In the euphoria of victory for the Allies, and the avoidance by Britain and the United States of the revolutions that occurred in Europe in the immediate post-war years, the distinction we now make between early and late First War poetry was blurred. Rupert Brooke's untimely death and attractive looks contributed to the enormous popularity of his poetry, with that poetry's simple message of the sacrifice of youth for the preservation of the righteous nation. The closing pages of Sassoon's volume of autobiography, *Siegfried's Journey, 1916–1920*, show how rapidly the effect of *his* war poetry faded once the war was over. I think perhaps that Sassoon and Owen didn't come fully into their own until the early Thirties. Following the publication of his *Collected Poems* in 1931 Owen gained the intense admiration of the new left-wing poets, evidenced by Auden's reference to him simply as 'Wilfred' in poem XVII of *Look, Stranger!* which first appeared in a periodical in 1933. I remember, too, poems by Owen and Sassoon being reprinted during the Thirties in the communist magazine *Left Review,* while in the March 1938 number of *New Verse,* by no means a Marxist periodical, there was a display page headed 'BE WARNED BY RUPERT BROOKE' and containing quotations from the poet's letters of 1913 and 1914. The page ended: 'Winston Churchill delivered a funeral oration over Brooke in *The Times.* The Old Fury is still under age for a funeral oration about you. TAKE CARE.' The Depression and the threat of a new war had put the poetry of the First War in a perspective whose lines now seem unlikely to be materially altered. In this the general acceptance by the intelligentsia of the revolutionary socialist view that the First War was, as Lenin said, 'a bourgeois-imperialist and dynastic war' played its part.

It's significant (though perhaps one shouldn't read too much into it) that in a less committed period, the recent past, there has been a revival of interest in Rupert Brooke. The publication of his letters in 1968 and the biographies by Christopher Hassall and Michael Hastings in 1964 and 1967 respectively, were by no means accompanied by the scathing tones used by *New Verse* in the Thirties. And, of course, the poetry of the First War has now become respectably ancient enough for academic studies, studies that tend inevitably to be conducted mainly in literary terms and to make theoretical cases. It is in fact a book by an American professor of English that I would like to use to articulate the necessarily brief survey of this poetry that time allows me. The book, *English Poetry of the First World War,* is by John H. Johnston and was published in 1964. It's quite a long book but its thesis is simple — that the poets of the First War were hampered in the expression and evaluation of their experience by their reliance on the lyric, but that there is in fact a clear evolutionary process towards the epic poem. Professor Johnston expounds this by a consideration of ten poets in turn — first, a group consisting of Rupert Brooke, Julian Grenfell, Robert Nichols and

Charles Sorley; then Sassoon, Edmund Blunden, Owen, Isaac
Rosenberg, Herbert Read and David Jones. One's only to utter
that sequence of names to see the plausibility of Professor
Johnston's argument, for which he also claims, justifiably I
believe, novelty. And whatever we may think of the illumination it finally provides, the argument certainly precludes desultori-
ness and dilettantism, twin perils of such a poetic survey — perils
which I am myself hoping to be saved from with Professor
Johnston's help. His thesis prevents detailed treatment of a few
poets who produced first-class work, notably Robert Graves and
Edgell Rickword, but this drawback we willingly accept in the
interests of a well-reasoned, well-shaped book. And also, since
the discussion of each poet dealt with has its eye on a conclusion,
we are constantly interested even when disagreeing.

For me, disagreement comes on two main points. First,
Professor Johnston takes for granted that the traditional virtues of
the epic poem survive into our times and are applicable to our
poetry. True, as he makes plain, the best of the First War poetry
persistently searches for perspectives longer than the personal
response to experience; true, that poetry is often helped to
greatness by narration, delineation of character, and the historical
view — indeed, I've been insisting myself on the importance of a
correct historical view. But we must doubt whether the mere
delineation of the two characteristics of the epic — the heroic
spirit and the detachment of the poet from personal involvement
— really take the thing higher where the poet himself has been
involved in the epic events. Of course, there is a sense in which
Hardy's poetic drama about the Napoleonic Wars, *The Dynasts,*
outclasses in power and range any other English poetry about
war, but Hardy was not writing about those events a year, five
years, twenty-five years after, but a hundred years. *The Dynasts*
is in no sense competing with, say, Coleridge's 'Fears in
Solitude', nor do its achievements make the contemporary
Napoleonic poem any less satisfactory. For Professor Johnston
the height of First War poetry is reached by David Jones's *In
Parenthesis* because it comes nearest to epic poetry, but one

trouble with that remarkable work is its ideology or, rather, lack of it. We are surely too conscious of the Marxist analysis of the First War to bear any retrospective treatment that doesn't take that analysis into account. Possibly at some future date an apparatus similar to the Phantom Intelligences that Hardy applied to the Napoleonic Wars could be successful, but I think that date is still far off. Again, Professor Johnston values Herbert Read's *The End of a War* as an important stage towards the epic, but its great drawback is its loss of temperature through the experiences recorded by the poem being invented, for though Read served with bravery in the war this poem is worked up from an incident he knew only at second-hand. It's interesting that Maurice Bowra even when examining the whole of European poetry of the First War (in the Taylorian Lecture of 1961) came to the conclusion that:

> The claim of the poets on posterity is that in their own special medium they made a brave attempt to grasp the war as they saw it. In its enormous monstrosity it could be understood only in fragments from individual angles through personal experience, and this is what the poets succeeded in doing, with truth and power. Modern war provides no material comparable with that of the *Iliad* or even of *Henry V*, and the poets have to take it as they find it. Their record of what they found has its own tragic distinction. They spoke for mankind in one of the cruellest ordeals to which it has ever been subjected, and their work bears testimony to what happens when malignant circumstances obliterate the familiar landmarks of civilization and rob man of his last assurance that anything in his existence is secure.

My other disagreement with Professor Johnston comes partly through his strict devotion to his thesis, partly because he is too narrowly sold on the Pound/Eliot revolution in poetic form and diction. For instance, since Edmund Blunden's war poetry was wider in range than Sassoon's, Professor Johnston sees him as a welcome further step along the road to the epic and so, in my opinion, over-values him. So that Professor Johnston hasn't a word of comment on the extraordinary non-language of a good deal of Blunden's war-time verse, of which I quote a fair specimen:

My soul, dread not the pestilence that hags
The valley; flinch not you, my body young,
At those great shouting smokes and snarling jags
Of fiery iron; as yet may not be flung
The dice that claims you.

Naturally, the 'advanced' form and diction of *In Parenthesis* only confirms Professor Johnston in the merits he finds in it on other grounds, for he sees it as paralleling other literary evolutionary experiments such as *Ulysses* and *The Waste Land*. But the work, whatever value may be given to it and whatever its typographical arrangement, is surely by and large in prose. I have never thought that its methods cast any doubt on the methods of the best of the First War poetry, or that they took the solution of the poetic problems arising out of the First War, or out of anything else, any distance at all. On the other hand it is a measure of Professor Johnston's fundamental sense and good taste that though a young poet killed in the war, Isaac Rosenberg, is tailor-made for a link in his chain of argument, and though he's inclined to over-praise him, too, the excessive rhetoric of that unhappy poet more often than not chokes in his gullet. Indeed, he has many acute passages of individual criticism. For example, he gives proper credit to the intelligent Charles Sorley who was killed in action before he had time to make his mark as a poet, but whose letters are essential to the period. He also shows precisely how Herbert Read's involvement in the theorizing that accompanied the Imagist movement let his personal war poetry down. Above all, his treatment of the poetry is always historical, and this is particularly enlightening in the cases of Sassoon and Owen.

Sassoon's evolution from a poet of conventional Georgian cast

is crucial. It needs a certain amount of actual testing of the stuff to
realize how bad a state English poetry was in immediately before
the First War. As T. S. Eliot wrote in 1954: 'The situation of
poetry in 1909 or 1910 was stagnant to a degree difficult for any
young poet of today to imagine.' One must emphasize that
Sassoon and, still more, Owen, were before their poems about
active service fixed in the dead post-Tennysonian tradition that
Eliot and Pound were in the secrecy of the *avant garde* in the
process of subverting. A more colloquial diction was forced on
Sassoon quite independently of the Eliot/Pound revolution. The
process is described in *Siegfried's Journey*, where he notes the satisfaction early in 1916 at 'introducing his Muse to the word
"frowst" ' and later of being the first writer 'to bring the word
"syphilitic" into the realm of English verse.'

> *The Bishop tells us: 'When the boys come back*
> *They will not be the same; for they'll have fought*
> *In a just cause: they lead the last attack*
> *On Anti-Christ; their comrade's blood has bought*
> *New right to breed an honourable race.*
> *They have challenged Death and dared him face to face.'*
>
> *'We're none of us the same!' the boys reply.*
> *'For George lost both his legs; and Bill's stone blind;*
> *Poor Jim's shot through the lungs and like to die;*
> *And Bert's gone syphilitic: you'll not find*
> *A chap who's served that hasn't found some change.'*
> *And the Bishop said: 'The ways of God are strange!'*

The new diction was passed on by Sassoon to Owen when the
two men met in the military hospital near Edinburgh, to which
they had both been sent suffering from what was then called
shell-shock or neurasthenia and now, I think, combat fatigue —
all euphemisms for the effect of modern war on the civilized
human. This meeting was as late as August 1917. It was here that
Owen as well as talking to Sassoon first read him in bulk and with
attention. Though Owen never in his own verse exploited the

savagely comic, the journalistic side of Sassoon, its example had the effect of reducing the mere poeticisms in Owen, of inducing greater realism and the realization that in the Wordsworthian sense his verse could speak to men. There is a significant footnote to a draft of his poem 'Spring Offensive', sent to Sassoon: 'Is this worth going on with? I don't want to write anything to which a soldier would say No Compris!' The other great lesson Owen learnt from Sassoon is summed up in a phrase spoken by the older poet which Owen quotes several times in his letters: 'Sweat your guts out writing poetry!' The astounding progress which Owen made as a poet during the last fifteen months of his life owes much to his pertinacity in carrying his poems through a large number of creatively progressive drafts.

One might interpolate here a word or two about the supposed reactionariness of the English verse tradition. There is no doubt that quite apart from the discoveries of the Americans towards the end of the first decade of this century, there had already been an English revolt against post-Tennysonian smoothness, poeticality and triviality. One need mention only the names of Hardy and Gerard Manley Hopkins. Hopkins's work was not fully revealed until after the First War, but poets like Sorley, Sassoon and Owen were sustained by Hardy's example and the last-named two poets took the style further. The line may be seen running again through Auden and other English Thirties poets, and later through Philip Larkin and some of the English Fifties poets. Though there are technical innovations in this poetry (such as what Owen called his 'vowel-rime stunt') it retains still the ancient resources of rhyme, stanza forms and stress metres, while trying to guard its diction from the artificially poetic. The effort is still worthwhile!

Professor Johnston's thesis naturally requires him to take a calm clear look at Owen, for though he is usually considered to be the best of the First War poets, his verse (apart from the fragmentary poem 'Strange Meeting') is very far from epic heroism, detachment and amplitude. Professor Johnston, taking his cue from Yeats's introduction to the *Oxford Book of Modern Verse*, first published in 1936, casts doubt on the adequacy of compassion as a poetic attitude. It will be remembered that Yeats had said that 'passive suffering is not a theme for poetry' and had excluded Owen from his anthology. Yeats was by no means on oath on this occasion and his remarks, it seems to me, were prompted mainly by political distaste for (and perhaps sexual prejudice against) the Thirties writers who had so enthusiastically taken Owen over and whom the reactionaries of the day were inclined to lump together, not only as communists but also as homosexuals. A similar though less violent prejudice may perhaps be detected in Dr Leavis who has suggested that Isaac Rosenberg rather than Owen is *the* poet of the First War. I myself see nothing against Owen as a 'sandwich-board Man of the revolution', which is how Yeats in a private letter later characterized him, but I think I can put that consideration aside in assessing his place.

Professor Johnston scarcely gives enough weight to the purely environmental difficulties affecting the war poet, and the neurotic sense he must have of swiftly passing opportunity. The forms of his poetry are foisted on him not so much by the lyrical tradition as by the sheer necessity to be brief. What more by way of talent could we have asked for Owen? No doubt, as Professor Johnston shows, he relies over-much on Christian symbolism: the political concepts of a poem such as 'Strange Meeting' are more telling.

> *For of my glee might many men have laughed,*
> *And of my weeping something had been left,*
> *Which must die now. I mean the truth untold,*
> *The pity of war, the pity war distilled.*
> *Now men will go content with what we spoiled,*
> *Or, discontent, boil bloody, and be spilled.*
> *They will be swift with swiftness of the tigress.*
> *None will break ranks, though nations trek from progress.*
> *Courage was mine, and I had mystery,*
> *Wisdom was mine, and I had mastery:*
> *To miss the march of this retreating world*
> *Into vain citadels that are not walled.*
> *Then, when much blood had clogged their chariot-wheels,*

I would go up and wash them from sweet wells,
Even with truths that lie too deep for taint.

Compassion — pity — in Owen's profound terms seems to me to make mincemeat of the attitudes adopted by the other poets singled out by Professor Johnston, always excepting Sassoon, whose work, on a rather lower level of ambition than Owen's, wears marvellously well and I'm sure will continue to do so. In the preface Owen drafted for the book of his poems that was not published in his lifetime he said: 'These elegies are to this generation in no sense consolatory. They may be to the next.' Alas, since Owen there has been no generation able to read with detachment his poetry of protest against war, of compassion for its victims.

I've already referred to the generation of Thirties poets to whose various angles of Marxist leanings the poetry of protest of the First War was an ideological support and, in the case of Owen, a source of technical inspiration and emotional tone. But the decade of the Thirties was momentous for its political complications and for the tergiversations of belief it induced, particularly among the middle-class intellectuals from whom, in Western society, poets largely spring. I suppose at the time of the Depression of 1929, when thoughts of a Second World War occurred, what was envisaged was a capitalist war against the Soviet Union, a renewal of the interventionist war of the period following the Bolshevik revolution. With the triumph of the Nazis the enemy began incredulously but more and more clearly to be seen as Germany, but as the decade wore on a strange ambiguity presented itself. The Moscow trials of some of the old Bolsheviks aroused a suspicion of the Soviet Union alarmingly reinforced by the Nazi-Soviet pact immediately before the outbreak of the Second War. Though continuing sympathizers with the Soviet Union could find good reasons for these events, the simple honeymoon period was over. And even when in September 1939 hostilities against Germany actually began, it seemed to some of us impossible that the capitalist powers would really carry through a war that would destroy the fascist régimes of Hitler and Mussolini, and so remove the menace to the Soviet Union.

History repeats itself, but the second time as farce: Marx's epigram must be very much in mind contemplating the Second War and the English poetry arising out of it. First of all, almost all the most celebrated poets of the Thirties avoided (I mean the verb to be neutral) active participation in it. Auden had gone to America before its outbreak; MacNeice, Spender and Day Lewis had or took civilian jobs that exempted them from service in the armed forces (though it should be mentioned that Spender was in the Auxiliary Fire Service in London). The poets who *were* called up felt by and large that the war was necessary to destroy fascism, but they had no enthusiasm or confidence about the governments that were to be the instrument for this. Patriotism was absent, but so too was indignation about horrors. Pacifism was an untenable position: equally so was a crusading spirit. Alun Lewis, one of the few outstanding poets of the Second War, has a remarkably accurate and vivid phrase in one of his letters for the mood induced; 'acceptance seems so spiritless, protest so vain'. On a general, perhaps rather superficial view, the values asserted by the English poetry of the Second War seem to be exclusively personal — an expression of sadness at the calamity that has befallen humanity, a nostalgia for the kindnesses and truths of domestic love. The virtue arising from the erotic affairs of two people — sometimes this seems to be all the poet is able to set against the disasters of a world. Even a poet like Randall Swingler, who retained his communist convictions throughout the Thirties and the war, appeals constantly to personal love: I quote from a poem of his written in 1943 during the invasion of Italy:

> O love! is it worth it? And are the dead rewarded
> With a bearer bond on history's doubtful balance?
> And is the loss redeemed by a sunset glory
> A sweet transfusion of blood to a new-born world?
>
> No, it will never be worth it, nor the loss redeemed.
> The dead die hideously and there is no honour.

The blood that runs out in the sand can only embitter
The violence of a fate that is still unmastered.

In those lines we see also what I think is the only widespread, non-private assertion in the poetry of the Second War: the idea that the soldier, the human unit, is worth more than the war, and that the unit has become inescapably involved in an inevitable convulsion. This is not the burning pacificism of the end of the First War: it is altogether more sullen and resigned, but in a queer way it does rise above the temporary historical considerations of its day, and I, for one, particularly in view of the way the world has gone since the Second War, have come to value it more than I did at the time.

I think there is no doubt, partly because of the abdication of the outstanding poets I have referred to, partly because of the ideological confusions, that no service poet emerged from the Second War of the order of Sassoon or Owen, nor does it seem very likely now that a participant will attempt a retrospective, more comprehensive work in the genre of Read's 'The End of a War' or Jones's *In Parenthesis*. The farcical-repetitious aspect of the Second War may also be seen in the journalistic cry which arose in its early days — 'Where are the war poets?' What was expected? A second Rupert Brooke, trumpeting the sad splendour of youth dying for its native land? As the so-called Phoney War ground on, a period when many of us more than half expected the British Government under Chamberlain to do a deal with Hitler, the question was answered by a civilian poet, C. Day Lewis, in a short poem actually called 'Where are the War Poets?'

They who in folly or mere greed
Enslaved religion, markets, laws,
Borrow our language now and bid
Us to speak up in freedom's cause.

It is the logic of our times,
No subject for immortal verse —

5

That we who lived by honest dreams
Defend the bad against the worse.

The comparative ease of avoidance by poets of active service, the change in the nature of warfare from the First War, the ideological disillusion are all amusingly shown by the reception of my own first wartime book of verse. When this was published in November 1942 (over three years after the start of the war) I was astonished to find a reviewer characterizing me as 'the only poet who has given us a clear picture of the life of the Forces'. That was quite an achievement, since only half the slim volume was written after I'd joined the Navy and half of that while I was merely under training.

No doubt, too, the critico-journalistic desire to find sacrificial victims led to the later elevation of Sidney Keyes as one of the two or three outstanding poets of the Second War, but oddly enough he was not, in the sense I've been using the term, really a war poet at all. He was an undergraduate here at Oxford until he entered the Army in April 1942, by which time he'd written about three quarters of all the poetry that has survived him. He served only five months in the ranks, and he must have spent several of them at an officers' training unit. He was killed in his first serious action. Not more than two of his poems are about his experience as a soldier.

In my view it was not until quite recently that the poetry of the Second War was put in a sound critical perspective, and this was due to a young critic, Ian Hamilton, who in 1965 published an anthology called *The Poetry of War 1939-45*, and in 1967 a selection from Alun Lewis's poetry and prose with a bio-graphical introduction. I want to refer in more detail to the latter book in a few moments. What Mr Hamilton did in the anthology seems very simple: just to apply sound standards of judgement to the muddled reputations and mass of material that came out of the Second War; but the notices of the anthology and other collec-tions that have appeared since show that for most critics the issues are still bedevilled by considerations other than those of poetic merit. One of the points made by Mr Hamilton's anthology is, as his introduction says, to show that the best poets of the Second War determined 'to be articulate and intelligible, a sensible participant, and to be scrupulous with language'—in other words, to carry into the next decade the best qualities of the poetry of the Thirties. The Forties have a bad poetic reputation: certainly the break-up of the Auden-dominated poetic movement at the start of the Second War admitted to power and publicity more of the romantic rhetoric that had been boiling up largely underground. But Mr Hamilton's anthology clearly shows that the significant poetry of the Second War is preponderantly 'in direct descent from Eliot and Auden' and 'attempted to confront a disintegrating world in personal terms that could make poetic sense out of it'.

The case of Keith Douglas, whose poetry is in my opinion the most brilliant achievement of all the service poets, is crucial to this view. Though he contributed to *New Verse*, the main organ of the Auden-dominated poets, while he was still at school, by the time he had come up here, to Oxford, in the autumn of 1938, there was a generation of poets which included many of vastly different aims from those of Auden and his followers, poets all too inclined to use a weaker language and a romantic apparatus, *Augury*, the 'Oxford Miscellany' published in 1940 which Douglas helped to edit, contains such Georgian atavism as:

> There is a place that to my private view
> More hallowed is than Athens or than Rome;
> An English house it is, an English home . . .

Those lines might have come from pre-Sassoon years. But Douglas's own poetry never quite lost, even in this Oxford period, what it had learnt from Auden in the Thirties (notably the non-Latinity of the earliest Auden), but some slush does break in—for example, a poem called 'Villanelle of Sunlight', dated 1940:

> O, sunlight settled on a wall
> Fills my heart with funerall [sic].

And Douglas caught at Oxford the infantile disease prevalent
there of using the adjective 'merry'—'with merry sound of splash
his weedy limbs' (this from a poem actually written after he joined
the Army). Had he not had the brain-power quickly to slough
off such influences the poetry he had so little time to write would
have greatly suffered, for it is the use of language at which he
excels (that, and his ear for natural but individual rhythm): his
ideology is practically non-existent and his observation constantly extending but not often remarkable. This absence of
superfluity is what makes his prose book, *Alamein to Zem Zem*,
extraordinary also: indeed, the interest in death, particularly its
physical manifestations, and in gross eating, or such things as a
flash of anti-semitism, are frequently too nakedly revealed for the
reader's comfort. (There is a romantic hangover here, too, in the
Alexandrian Quartet-type character of Milena.) But even in North
Africa his poetry doesn't, I think, make a great, or even a wholly
satisfactory statement: his most successful poems are in fact among
the non-active service poems. He remains, one thinks, closing the
Collected Poems, a poet of tremendous promise.

However much one admires his talent and the drive that
enabled him to produce so much work under such distracting
conditions, he was never faced, hadn't by the time of his death in
Normandy in 1944 at the age of twenty-four felt the need to face,
any of those problems of organic development as a writer, as a
man, that faced the other outstanding poet of the Second War,
Alun Lewis. Lewis's work is far more uneven than Douglas's, but
despite its weaknesses its scope is wider and more deeply human.
I must confess that I've been helped to this view of Lewis by the
selection of his work made and introduced by Ian Hamilton which
I've already mentioned. To many like myself, whose roots were
in the Thirties, the main point about Lewis seemed the sense that
his last poems, written in India, were an abdication from the
responsibility of making a poetic statement about oppression and
hope, about the soldier's life and the issues of the war:

. . . we who dream beside this jungle pool
Prefer the instinctive rightness of the poised
Pied kingfisher deep darting for a fish
To all the banal rectitude of states,
The dew-bright diamonds on a viper's back
To the slow poison of a meaning lost
And the vituperations of the just.

One felt about those lines that the 'preferences' for nature or instinct meant that the poet had abandoned humanity and was incapable of saying anything meaningful about the human activities in which he was playing a part. Lewis's death on active service in 1944 seemed part of the same process, for there were rumours that the shot that caused it was self-inflicted. The responsibility of making a comprehensive poetic statement was all the heavier for Lewis because of his acute sense, right from the start of his call-up into the Army, of his great and more innocent ancestors of the First War, particularly Edward Thomas. The best of his earlier poems, such as 'Odi et Amo', are a brave though far from wholly successful attempt to contrive something as universal as Owen's poetry out of the training and English camp life of the Phoney War:

My body does not seem my own
Now. These hands are not my own
That touch the hair-spring trigger, nor my eyes

Fixed on a human target, nor my cheek
Stroking the rifle butt; my loins
Are flat and closed like a child's.

But one of the virtues of Mr Hamilton's introduction to his book of Lewis selections, is its demonstration that Lewis's development towards an interior poetry was not merely a result of taking a commission or the confusion of war aims and wartime alliances or a failure of nerve (though such crudities no doubt played their part). It arose from his essential poetic personality; indeed it arose from an essential need (which it was evidence of talent in Lewis to find objective correlatives for in the physical circumstances in which he was placed) to deepen and strengthen his verse. His turning, on his voyage to India, to Rilke is a crucial example of this. Probably many poets of the Second War got hold of the little Leishman-translated selected Rilke which came out in the New Hogarth Library in 1941 (and one would guess that this was Lewis's immediate source), but few or none save Lewis were then able to make use of it. Before coming to the key lines of Lewis's poem 'To Rilke', Mr Hamilton quotes two passages from Lewis's journal of the time about a strange dream, and then about Lewis's reading of the German poet: 'He approached me as we were lying off India and I asked him about *silence*, and what price one paid for going my way—through the panzer divisions of the century—and whether he would have found his silence there . . .' This expository treatment by Mr Hamilton is especially illuminating with Lewis, partly because of his immaturities (the prose needs reinforcing with the verse, and sometimes the other way about) and partly because the tone of the verse is so quiet that we are apt to miss its implications:

> *Rilke, if you had known that I was trying*
> *To speak to you perhaps you would have said*
> *'Humanity has her darlings to whom she's entrusted*
> *A farthing maybe, or a jewel, at least a perception*
> *Of what can develop and what must always be endured*
> *And what the live may answer to the dead.*
> *Such ones are known by their faces,*
> *At least their absence is noted;*
> *And they never lack an occasion,*
> *They, the devoted.'*

Lewis was twenty-eight when he died, older than Owen and Douglas, already facing and interestingly grappling with the problems that face every poet as he emerges from his youth. It may be that had he lived he would have moved more into the field of

prose fiction—he was an excellent letter-writer and was already
the author of some short stories of actually greater human range
than his verse.

Preparing this lecture, reading again some of the poetry of war,
long familiar, I've been moved not only by the waste of talent but
also by the reiteration by so many poets, often scarcely out of their
boyhood, of the essential brotherhood of mankind, and of the
brotherhood, too, of poets and their audience. What a marvellous
and tragic literature this is, the best of it; in the end beyond critical
carping and judicious placing, reflecting the human spirit that we
hope—that we must believe—will rescue us from the disasters
inherent in history and the outworn systems in which we are
shackled, from all the ways that, in Owen's words, 'nations trek
from progress'. And I must also add that the essential message of this
poetry more and more strikes home to me—cutting across theories
of just wars, defensive wars, liberatory wars—the message that
the killing of one human by another is an evil incapable of justification or expiation. In India Alun Lewis turned down the offer
of an instructor's job to stay with his battalion on active service—
'for two reasons', as he said in a letter—'to have authority in the
long fight for peace and to share the comradeship of war, and of
death'. Even in the context of the Second War and of his own fate
one doesn't feel the remark was made in vain.

I seem to recall that it was Stephen Spender who some time in the
Thirties said that the opposite of poetry was not prose but war—a
romantic aphorism, but one whose implications have deepened
since it was uttered. Poetry in this century has come to be more
widely regarded as the one human discourse of integrity, completeness, truth. A major criterion of its value is, rightly in my opinion,
taken to be the extent to which it embodies such qualities. This
kind of direct importance of poetry (which expressed before 1914,
by Matthew Arnold say, seems somewhat theoretical) has been
clarified by the reaction of poets to war, the reaction of the par-
ticipants in the First War, the Spanish Civil War, the Second War;
the assertion of the values of culture at the gravest moments of
culture's crisis.

VIII

Poetic Memories
of the Thirties

In the Summer of 1970 I took part in a symposium about Thirties
poetry at the Mermaid Theatre with John Lehmann, Jack Lindsay,
Stephen Spender and Julian Symons. All of us had lived through
the period as young men and contributed in varying degrees to its
verse. There was nearly a full house, and Stephen Spender said to
me at the interval how surprised he was at the size of the audience
and the interest it showed. 'Imagine,' he said, 'if in the Thirties
there'd been a symposium of Nineties poets. We wouldn't have
crossed the street to hear them.' The thought is quite a striking one.
We were then as far from the 1930s as the Thirties were from the
1890s. If any young poets of the Thirties had an interest in Lionel
Johnson or Ernest Dowson or John Davidson it was merely, I
think, an Eng. Lit. interest. It's not without point to recall that
Julian Symons's elder brother, A. J. A. Symons, the biographer of
Baron Corvo, in fact published an anthology of Nineties verse in
1928, a year when from private presses and in university publications the Thirties poets were beginning to emerge. The anthology
was an excellent one, reviving a number of half-forgotten names,
but of course it fell on stony ground so far as the preoccupations
of the then aspiring young poets were concerned. The interest in

Thirties poetry today is rather more than an antiquarian one, though probably there is an element in it, when the survivors of that period actually appear before an audience, of morbid or geriatric curiosity.

I think the main interest is ideological, though there is also a technical one. Perhaps neither is ever very clearly felt or expressed; and whether the personal view I'm going to give will add any clarity is also doubtful. The ideological interest has elements of nostalgia. The Thirties were a time when the brotherhood of man was not only believed in but seemed capable of practical achievement. The labour movement, despite its weaknesses, divisions and confusions, couldn't be regarded as other than international in scope. The crises of the times were such as to seem to require a social revolution to cure. For many, a way to such revolution could be seen first through the united front of left and right in the labour movement, and then through the broader-based popular front. Poets envisaged a growing audience whose ideals were social justice; and they tried to bring into their verse a subject matter of real concern to such an audience.

On the technical side of poetry the Thirties were well placed. The Eliot/Pound revolution in the language and rhythms of poetry (and, to an extent, in the content of poetry) had cleared away, for many young poets, the stagnant tradition left in England when the exoticism of the Nineties had collapsed. The new young poets were lucky enough to have in W. H. Auden a leader who showed, right from the start, that the traditional resources of English verse could be used for a poetry just as free, as 'contemporary', and as broad and penetrating as that encompassed by the freer forms of the two Americans.

My own modest entry into the ranks of the Thirties poets was scarcely typical (like some army composed mainly of officers, recruitment was largely from Oxbridge) but it shows how compelling was the style and ethos of the new movement. In 1928, when I was sixteen, I bought Ezra Pound's *Selected Poems*, then just published, edited and introduced by T. S. Eliot. At the same time a school friend bought Eliot's *Poems 1909–1925*. Ordering these volumes from our provincial bookshop, we were conscious of taking a revolutionary step in our self-education, but now it seems to me not very likely that we'd any proper grasp of the revolution evidenced by the books. It was Eliot's sordid passages that excited us, the 'clasping the yellow soles of feet / In the palms of both soiled hands' business; and also what we thought of in those non-permissive days as the 'shocking' quatrains:

Grishkin is nice: her Russian eye
Is underlined for emphasis;
Uncorseted, her friendly bust
Gives promise of pneumatic bliss.

Quite a lot of Pound's 1928 Selected Poems is in his post-Rossetti, post-Browning style, not uncongenial to me then but seemingly irrelevant to the concept of poetry as something to blow up the Philistines with. I suppose what impressed me most about Pound was his free verse, particularly the short, epigrammatic pieces, and Eliot's grave pronouncements about free verse in his introduction to the selection. 'No vers is libre,' said Eliot, 'to the man who wants to do a good job.' That was immensely reassuring for even at that tender age I'd sensed the difficulties inherent in free verse—that though it helps one to escape from mere 'poetical' language and rhythms, its texture tends to be poverty-stricken and its procedures frighteningly arbitrary. Remember that there was already a tradition of free verse in English poetry, with which I had some faint familiarity. Matthew Arnold's experiments were unknown to me, I'm sure, but I'd read odd poems by such as W. E. Henley, and this kind of free verse line was continued into the Twenties by poets like Osbert Sitwell who influenced me a good deal at that time. But all this was very different from Eliot actually categorizing and evaluating various kinds of free verse, with reference to such matters as the speaking tones of Browning's blank verse and the technical looseness of the Jacobean dramatists.

As I've said, by 1928 the later revolution in poetry had already started, unknown to us in our provincial petty-bourgeois existence.

When it broke in on me it had far more practical immediacy than
the revolution of Eliot and Pound. The latter poets, as already
indicated, had revolted against the dead diction, the constricted
subject matter of the first two decades of the century. The revolution at the end of the Twenties took the gains of that revolt for
granted. It's somewhat curious that new movements in poetry
often seem initially to be primarily about extensions in subject
matter. Despite what Eliot had done for yellow feet and pneumatic busts, the new Thirties poets did appear—and not merely
to a more or less simple public of poetry readers—before all else
to be bringing into poetry with freshness, ease and stunning effect
the properties of ordinary modern life. There is an example from a
book published by C. Day Lewis in 1931 that still seems to me
startling and amusing—the idea that spring is signalled by
gasometers rising because less gas is used in warmer weather:

> To-day crowds quicken in a street,
> The fish leaps in the flood:
> Look there, gasometer rises,
> And here bough swells to bud.

But of course the deeper note struck by the new poetry was its
condemnation of the waste of men and resources in the crisis that
had come over the capitalist world, and the corollary belief that
the crisis could be solved only by a socialist revolution.

In the summer of 1930, by an odd stroke of luck, I met the critic
John Davenport, then an undergraduate, who had just helped to
edit *Cambridge Poetry 1929*, which contained poems by himself,
John Lehmann, William Empson, and others. He also told me
about the young Oxford poets; about Auden's 1930 *Poems*, then
just published, and about another poet who was going to be good
but who hadn't yet published a book, Stephen Spender. From the
same small-town bookshop I ordered the Auden volume, for-
tunately priced modestly at half-a-crown, and *Oxford Poetry 1930*,
which included five poems by Spender, astonishing as the work of
an undergraduate. They are well worth looking at today, though

finding them all is another matter. The poem 'Souvenir de Londres' appeared in Spender's 1933 *Poems*, without the title, as poem XI, but he dropped it from his *Collected Poems* (1955)*. It's written in rhymed quatrains, under the influence of the Jacobeans via T. S. Eliot. If I read the first two stanzas I think it may be seen that Spender perhaps never later used strict prosodic forms with greater success, nor did he really go on to exploit the splendid mix of formal language and personal experience:

My parents quarrel in the neighbour room:—
'How did you sleep last night?' 'I woke at four
To hear the wind that sulks along the floor
Blowing up dust like ashes from the tomb.'

'I was awake at three.' 'I heard the moth
Breed perilous worms.' 'I wept
All night, watching your rest.' 'I never slept
Nor sleep at all.' Thus ghastly they speak, both.

One might say of this poem that it was uncharacteristic Thirties poetry. But I hope what will emerge as we go on is some indication of the variety of work the period produced. Another of these *Oxford Poetry* pieces Spender later put in more general terms and, I believe, rather spoilt. He removed the naïveties of the poem but also a good deal of its fresh feeling about what is certainly a characteristic theme of the times, unemployment. In particular, the final image of the poem disappeared, possibly because the poet grew to feel it to be too esoteric. A favourite brand of cigarette of the day was Gold Flake, which came in a buttercup-yellow packet, white on the inside. Here are the last two stanzas of the original version of the poem. The poet is addressing an out-of-work friend:

Nor shall I ever fail to see
One photographic memory,
Of how, still leaning on a post,
You stride the gutter where men spit,

* It is in the *Selected Poems*.

And, laughing loudly, we both look
Down on a torn and yellow box.
For on my brain I felt impress
That white, appalling emptiness.

The early Spender exerted an enormous fascination. The great gift for phrase-making and individual rhythm marks almost every poem in the collection of 1933. Even the occasional unclarities and bafflements seemed to be meaningful. For some time this poetry has been known through the revised version of it Spender made for his *Collected Poems*, so that its original impact has been even harder to recapture. I'd like to quote the original ending of poem XXXII in the 1933 *Poems*, the splendid address to time. In the revised version the words 'larger', 'particular', 'progress' and 'huge' have disappeared: 'those stellar shores' has become 'the stellar shores'; and in the last line there is no haunting repetition of 'distant' and 'worlds' and 'world'. There is a certain gain in clarity, particularly on one point of punctuation, but a sad loss of musicality and specificness, and something of that ambitiousness of utterance so characteristic of the Thirties:

Our universal ally, but larger than our purpose, whose flanks
Stretch to planets unknown in our brief, particular battle,
Tomorrow Time's progress will forget us even here,
When our bodies are rejected like the beetle's shard, today
Already, now, we are forgotten on those stellar shores.
Time's ambition, huge as space, will hang its flags
In distant worlds, and in years on this world as distant.

The personal and political sides of Spender came together in a long poem called *Vienna* which he published in 1934. It's about the abortive rising of the Viennese workers against the fascist régime of Dolfuss. It was never reprinted and I suppose is now almost unknown except to survivors or specialists of the period. I was a sturdy defender of the poem at its time of publication (not least because I conceived that those attacking it lacked sympathy for the revolutionary cause) but now I'm forced to agree with most of its reviewers that it is not successful. What it demonstrated for me at the time, more compellingly, I think, than any other work of the period, was how a long political poem might be written. The passages of fact, satire and narration are integrated into the essential personal lyricism of the whole, so that the thing is direct but not crudely propagandist. And many of the lines provided models of imagery, tone and rhythm that have gone on influencing me. To extract bleeding chunks from the poem would do it great damage. but not to be too tantalizing about it perhaps I ought to quote a few lines. These depict the thoughts of the socialists imprisoned after the fighting:

> There are some flowers spring in our memory
> There are some birds that cut the bare sky.
> We in prison meditate much on the rare gentian
> Are terrible in our envy of the beasts' freedom
> Become dangerous as birds, as flowers. The dead, as stones.
> Rosa Luxemburg wished finally to be a bird,
> Watched grasses and dreamt of orchids. Uttermost life is birds
> Or undying anemone, as the dying man saying
> 'Here the insurrection ends, here revolution begins.'
> His saying this, not dying. Also amongst those
> The sulky heifer, the furnished goat, Fey's swine,
> Who dared not even shoot, whose 'special tasks'
> Were hanging, finishing off the wounded, insulting
> The corpses in the street with placards
> 'Here lies the handiwork of your leaders.'

In a way, *Vienna* was the period's most complete fusion of poetic talent with political rhetoric, though of course it scarcely begins to solve one of the greatest problems of Thirties poetry, the problem of how a poet of one class could write for another class. It may not be clear today how variously their communist sympathies or beliefs affected the lives and work of the poets of the period. There was first an opposition between those whose communism, either through actual membership of the Communist Party, or through rigid principles, dictated stringently the content and manner of their verse, and those who, despite their left-wing alignment, kept a greater poetic licence. The complicated sub-divisions of these two main groups would be difficult to distinguish now: a look merely at the biographies and work of those five of us at the Mermaid Theatre symposium would be an indication of the discriminations involved. Perhaps it can be said that as the Thirties wore on the interesting names by and large went their own ways — in Spender's case, indeed, fairly soon into a very personal and inward poetry. But though the non-Oxbridge names saw themselves on the whole as opposed to the Oxbridge names, former membership of the two ancient universities was by no means a passport out of the ranks of the committed. C. Day Lewis's poetry, for instance, continued to battle with the hard problems of attempted mass communication and a content as relevant to the times as a political pamphlet: however, I myself wrote a very rude notice of a collection of his in 1938 — I was ideologically at one with him but I had some impossibly idealistic notion of what sort of poetry might come out of his commitment. His friend, Rex Warner, also kept along the socialist line and his collection of the previous year found rather more favour with me, perhaps because some of the poems dealt with a colonial scene, with less obvious ideological targets. But despite my scepticism about such honest work, I suppose it was a good time after the epoch ended that I could smile without indignation at Cyril Connolly's parodies of Oxbridge left-wing verse:

M is for Marx
and Movement of Masses
and Massing of Arses
and Clashing of Classes.

What may be described as the orthodox communist verse of the period is now virtually lost, sunk by its crudity of technique and weight of rhetoric. The obvious exception to such an unkind generalization is John Cornford. He was killed in the Spanish Civil War at the age of twenty-one, so that despite his precocity we have to remember that in considering his poetry we are considering juvenilia. He too was an Oxbridge poet, but of a later generation, and though his schoolboy poems are heavily indebted to Auden, as a Cambridge undergraduate he was already rejecting, as well as the Eliot tradition, the private and emotional leftness of the Auden group—and also the surrealism that by then had crossed the Channel. All this is amusingly shown by a squib he wrote for an undergraduate magazine, called 'Keep Culture out of Cambridge':

> *Wind from the dead land, hollow men,*
> *Webster's skull and Eliot's pen,*
> *The important words that come between*
> *The unhappy eye and the difficult scene.*
> *All the obscene important names*
> *For silly griefs and silly shames,*
> *All the tricks we once thought smart,*
> *The kestrel joy and the change of heart,*
> *The dark mysterious urge of the blood,*
> *The donkeys shitting on Dali's food,*
> *There's none of these fashions have come to stay,*
> *And there's nobody here got time to play.*
> *All we've brought are our party cards*
> *Which are no bloody good for your bloody charades.*

In the poem Cornford wrote in Spain called 'Full Moon at Tierz: Before the Storming of Huesca', his political convictions—commonplace though they are in the context of the period—are conveyed with extraordinary purity and intensity. Also some sure instinct prompted him to write the poem in rhymed stanzas, though the circumstances of its composition must have been against this, and, indeed, further drafts could easily have removed some awkwardness. I needn't read from it: Cornford was one poet of the times who couldn't later change or suppress his work, and the poem is familiar through anthologies.

I can't read the poem aloud without emotion. I'm sure I admire it more now than when I first read it, though it made with urgency and clarity the sort of statements I'd been fumbling for myself not many years before. For even as it was being written, the issues, both literary and political, that had seemed so clear-cut at the start of the Thirties were already, for many, becoming complicated. Perhaps, indeed, for the bourgeois poet his position was really only simple at the moment when the truths of scientific socialism presented themselves, and the practical question arose of 'going over' to the working-class. In my own case the accident of a change of job and residence in the mid-Thirties took me out of an involvement in local politics and left me with a largely theoretical concern with commitment, until the Second World War started and everyone was, in a way, committed practically. But I want to come back at the end to the relation of politics and art as exemplified in the life of the individual.

It would need a separate discussion to deal with the question of which was closer to proletarian art, Cornford's inspired versification of political slogans in his Huesca poem or a piece like Spender's 'A Footnote'. The latter has the sub-title 'From Marx's Chapter on The Working Day', and what Spender did was to adapt and arrange extracts from Factory Inspectors' reports and so forth, quoted by Marx, and then add a lyrical commentary of his own. Again, this is a poem I can't hear today without being moved. Quite apart from the poem's merit, there's something touching in the idea of a young middle-class poet ploughing (or starting to plough) through *Das Kapital* and making a poem out of the experience. But the various recipes for socialist writing, and the reservations about the entire concept, so urgent at the time, have been succeeded simply by the question of which writing was good and which was less good. Each epoch has its gritty problems of truly depicting itself and only in retrospect perhaps can we say that one strategy had its advantage over another.

All the same, it's interesting that the work of the other fine English poet killed in Spain, Christopher Caudwell, belongs to the unsectarian branch of left-wing Thirties verse, though he was a notable Marxist theorist and devoted to the humble day-to-day tasks of a Communist Party member. At the time one knew only a few of his poems, from their appearance in periodicals, because they weren't collected until the end of the period, but one now sees his death as a considerable casualty to English poetry. It was a casualty, too, to science, literary criticism, straight fiction and crime fiction, engineering and aeronautics, to all of which this extra-ordinary young man made unusual contributions. In his verse his Marxism is ordinarily in the background. For instance, the attitude of mind in his poem 'Tierra del Fuego' is against early colonialism and the cruelties of dogmatic religion, but though the ideology articulates the poem it is subservient to the richness of the language and the resourcefulness in sketching in the characters and ambience of the Spanish conquerors. Again, a poem called 'The Stones of Ruskin' ends with an account of the various fates of the poet in society. No doubt the society is bourgeois society, and no doubt the weaknesses of the poetic character are also in question, but Caudwell was wise enough to keep the business open and general:

> Some few in garrets starved or blue gulfs drowned
> Are lucky ones, taken in youthful bloom.
> Some in dress suits, protective mimicry,
> Succeed in imitating business men
> And the hawk Furies baffled pass them over.
> The wisest stop their gambols and become
> As ease stops up the operative glands
> Sleek, ox-eyed, ruminative gelded beasts
> Or at the worst drift off the stage of life
> The slobber-lipped and palsied clowns of age.
> And others come to curse the thing they blessed
> And daub their chains with filth or scream at night
> Whipped by all the fat devils out of hell
> Until their brother-madmen stop their mouths.

In the introduction to his excellent Penguin anthology, *Poetry of the Thirties*, Robin Skelton has an interesting few pages on what he calls the 'irrational, nightmarish, outrageously introverted poetry' that the younger poets began to produce in the middle of the decade. Like all historical summaries, his view doesn't precisely accord with one's actual experience, but then one is oneself speaking now long after the experience, with all the loss of nuance that implies. I'm sure my own divorce from practical politics encouraged the abandonment of a dry puritanical didacticism. But I think in any case I wouldn't have seen in the strictly Marxist sides of Day Lewis or Cornford any viable recipe for the poetry demanded by the age, still less in the political poetry of lesser left-wing poets. When surrealism arrived, in about 1935, imported by almost a one-man firm, the precociously brilliant David Gascoyne, it gave sanction to the way things were already going. It could be used, like a patent muscle-exerciser, as a means of loosening up one's verse. But the seeds of the fantastic had been implanted early in the poetry of the decade. Auden's *The Orators* of 1932 was a very influential book, and I read many passages in it as if they were surrealist, though now they seem (as they were in fact) simply examples of Auden's generalizing power and intellectual curiosity:

> One delivers buns in a van, halting at houses. One can amend a mutilated text; one can estimate the percentage of moisture in a sample of nitre. One decorates a room for a lady in black and silver; one manufactures elephant drums for a circus.

It's hard indeed to recover one's attitude to the spate of poetry in which one was so completely immersed. But certainly at the start of the period one disapproved of the public school and university chumminess that sometimes accompanied the left-wing poetry. And at the end of the period one disapproved even more of the personal romanticism and reckless obscurity represented by one side of Dylan Thomas's verse. One was searching, hopelessly it seems now, for a poetry with impeccable political orientation, yet as rich and free as the great English poetry of the past.

It must have been lack of sympathy with the liberal scepticism behind Louis MacNeice's poetry that made me undervalue it at the time. His work of the Thirties has worn extremely well, and so, I believe, has the work of lesser poets who shared with him what may be described as neutral ground—I think particularly of Kenneth Allott and Bernard Spencer. Looking back, I regret not taking more to heart the lessons their poetry provides, though I pinched a few things from them at the time.

I certainly pinched from Norman Cameron, who strangely enough was largely unpolitical and technically non-experimental. He had appeared, fully armed as a poet, in the volumes of *Oxford Poetry* which came out a few years before 1930. His poetry patently derives from that of Robert Graves, but as so often in art it was the imitator rather than the originator that one found it useful to imitate. However, to call Cameron an imitator of Graves is to do him injustice. He developed and refined one side of Graves, and so became the true source of the many brief mythologico-anecdotal poems written in the Thirties. What could be taken from Cameron was really a trick of constructing a poem with shape, concrete properties, and point. The trick could be used for purposes other than Cameron's own moral and historical ambiguities, but often his imitators lost in the process his naturalness and bite. Only when one has tried to do the thing oneself does one realize what an adroit and imaginative talent he had. The poetry he fathered often survives when more ambitious but clotted productions have become unreadable. He was a manageable influence where very often Auden was not.

From Auden, as from a schoolboy hero, one took a tone of voice, catch phrases, beliefs—the very cut of one's poetic personality. His 1930 *Poems* is a marvellous and various collection: much time would be needed to try to show its effect on the ensuing decade. What I would single out now was the heroic tone in face of a disastrous time, a tone so characteristic of the early Thirties and appearing even more markedly in Auden-influenced poets like Day Lewis and Rex Warner. The heroics couldn't be sustained against the ideological confusions and historical disappointments that were to come, but they weren't false heroics and were, in part at least, truly earned by the actions of some poets in the Spanish Civil War and by less sensational service to their fellow men through modest activities in the labour movement. Compared with the Eliot-dominated pessimism of the Twenties, a dramatic change had come over English poetry.

But the Auden of the mid-Thirties had a still greater fascination for young poets. His poetry quickly gained clarity, and its confident summations and even its flowing lyricism didn't lack critics who saw a falling-off from the knotted, Delphic, obscurely personal utterances of the earliest work. Such scruples have lost a good deal of relevance now the period has sunk back into history and Auden himself has developed a succession of styles and a splendidly copious *oeuvre*. I myself had a few doubts about the way he was going in the later Thirties, but they were as nothing beside the excitement felt in the presence of a great and congenial contemporary talent. I recover some of that excitement when I look again at the five love sonnets he published in the little poetry magazine *New Verse* in 1933. They were obviously written after reading Shakespeare's—one more example of his practical demonstrations that the traditional forms of English poetry were not necessarily reactionary. He must have come to regard the sequence as too self-revelatory or perhaps incompletely successful, for the first four were never reprinted. Even if one hears just the octave of the first sonnet I think the attraction of this manner of Auden's can be plainly felt. The beauty of the iambics is obvious; and pointing the amatory theme are characteristic and appealing references—to the poverty of the time and to the psycho-analytical theory of sublimation. The adjective 'preposterous' is typical of several Audenesque epithets that poets of the age caught as easily as a common cold (though presumably Auden had taken the word from Shakespeare's Sonnet 109 and typically made it his own):

Sleep on beside me though I wake for you:
Stretch not your hands towards your harm and me,
Lest, waking, you should feel the need I do
To offer love's preposterous guarantee
That the stars watch us, that there are no poor,
No boyish weakness justifying scorn;

To cancel off from the forgotten score
The foiled caresses from which thought was born.

Literary histories of the Thirties have already been written, are in the process of being written, by those who never experienced the decade. Sometimes one's consulted on matters of mood or factual detail. My own memory is an utterly fallible instrument, but even those with better recall can often err at this distance from events. Moreover, any contributions by the survivors will, on the whole, do little to affect the theories and narratives of literary historians coming after. Their processes are, I suppose inevitably, of a neatening and rationalizing kind. The personal biography and the precise class position of the writers, as well as every word they wrote, played a part in making the epoch, and of course such things are virtually irrecoverable.

There is a single work, however, essential to an understanding of the period, and that is Edward Upward's fictional trilogy, of which at the moment two volumes have appeared. Upward's role in the new literary movement at the start of the Thirties is now well known. He is the character called 'Chalmers' in Christopher Isherwood's autobiographical book of 1938, *Lions and Shadows*. He contributed two remarkable short stories to the seminal anthology *New Country* of 1933 and a long extract from a novel in the first number of *New Writing* in 1936. He worked as a schoolmaster until his retirement at normal age limit, and was a member of the Communist Party throughout the Thirties and far beyond. He seems to have abandoned imaginative writing some time during the second half of the Thirties. Certainly he published nothing of that kind for twenty years.

His novel *In the Thirties*, the first volume of the trilogy, is mainly a phenomenally accurate reconstruction of the political life of a middle-class married couple as orthodox communists in the Thirties. Not only is the atmosphere of the period meticulously conveyed but also, and more important, the niceties of ideological argument against the events of the time. The book was hailed on its appearance in 1962 by several makers of the Thirties literature, notably John Lehmann, Christopher Isherwood and Stephen Spender, but the ordinary reader may wonder somewhat at their enthusiasm. The style of the novel, though clear, is extraordinarily dry. Irony may sometimes be suspected but I'm sure is not there. Neither is any Dickensian or other exaggeration of character, nor any undue drama in the incidents related. I think the restraint displayed by Upward is hardly to be understood until the second volume, called *The Rotten Elements*, is read. This book is set in the late 1940s, when the same middle-class couple begin to question the political line of the Communist Party. Simultaneously, the man, Alan Sebrill, starts to feel that he may once again write the poetry that during his whole political activity he has suppressed—suppressed not only because devotion to it would have diverted him from the political struggle but also because he had previously felt poetic activity to be in itself a remnant of his bourgeois nature, and therefore a weakness.

The Rotten Elements is largely as dry and restrained as *In the Thirties*, but because of the hero's reflections on poetry in relation to politics and his own life, the book acquires an extraordinary second dimension. Though the Thirties in England weren't without opportunities for extreme political commitment and though many English men and women saw active service during the ensuing World War, we have suffered no repressive régime nor, despite air raids, any catastrophe from without. We can't expect from our novelists a *Doctor Zhivago*, say. It seems to me, however, that Edward Upward's trilogy will be seen, despite its small scale, to be a work of that order. It is most germane to my main theme and elevates it to a plane above but parallel to the personal theme I've been attempting to delineate. Early in *The Rotten Elements* comes a passage which I must quote in full: Alan Sebrill's thoughts about the relation of poetry to politics:

He was filled with the conviction, as he had often been in the past, that poetic creation was what his nature needed and ought not to be deprived of. 'At last I have come alive again,' he found himself thinking, 'after years of political activity.'

But immediately he took alarm. To have had such a thought indicated a serious deterioration in his attitude towards the Party. What sort of poetically creative mood was this that had brought him to the verge of revulsion against the necessary day-to-day work which as a Party member he ought always to be eager to do? It was a would-be deserter's mood, wholly impermissible, it was the mood of some renegade-in-the-making, capriciously weary of the door-to-door canvassing, the jumble sales, the small public meetings, all the unspectacular duties that must unceasingly be performed at this stage of the struggle for the future happiness of humanity. And yet, how much more gladly—how much more effectively even—he would have done his Party work during recent years if only he had been able in his spare time to write poetry. How much more gladly he would have been able to do it from now on if only the creative mood that had just come upon him had been of a kind he could have allowed himself to continue to indulge in.

. . . He had the sudden hope that his poetic excitement might when fully understood prove to be pro-Party after all. Perhaps it was not antagonistic to his everyday Party activities except in so far as these had tended to be zestless during the years when he had written no poetry. In fact, what it might be urgently telling him was that his political work needed the re-invigoration which only his return to poetry-writing could give. This idea, as soon as it occurred to him, seemed valid. His poetic excitement, no longer suspect, was released from the restraint his Party conscience had put upon it.

No doubt the hero's scruples as expressed here are uncommon, even neurotic. But the themes discussed underlie the poetry of the Thirties and perhaps are again beginning to underlie the poetry of today. Later in the book, thinking about the possible subjects of the poetry he wants to write, Alan Sebrill reflects:

His intending it to convey a political messaeg had certainly not been wrong. What other motive could he justifiably have for wanting to write a poem? If, in this age of Auschwitz and

Hiroshima and of the still greater horrors imperialism was preparing to inflict on the world, he wanted to write poetry for its
own sake, or for his own sake, or in the contemptible and ridiculous hope of making himself famous, or for any purpose except
to support the struggle against imperialism—then he was little
better than those bandsmen who when new batches of victims
were brought to the Nazi extermination camps welcomed them
with classical music in order to lull their fears and to keep them
docile.

Most of the preoccupations of the essential Thirties poetry are
here expressed—perhaps with a degree of naïvety but with rare
and moving honesty. In particular it shouldn't be forgotten that
the members of the middle-class who joined the parties of the Left
did so to try to ensure, in Upward's words, 'the future happiness of
humanity'. Nor has the prime requirement of the Thirties really
changed, so far as poets feel in their bones that poetry ought somehow to be in the service of that humanity, and that politics should
be as truthful as poetry.

IX

The Planet on the Table

'Others abide our question.' For years I completely failed to understand this opening sentence of Matthew Arnold's sonnet on Shakespeare. Of course, the poem immediately goes on to make its general situation plain:

> *Others abide our question. Thou art free.*
> *We ask and ask— Thou smilest and art still,*
> *Out-topping knowledge.*

But, I wondered, what was the question Arnold was putting to Shakespeare and other poets? A note in Kenneth Allott's* masterly edition of Arnold's poems gives one answer: the note is a quotation from a book by Schiller, which I suppose Arnold may have read: 'Since I was accustomed by the practice of modern poets to seek the poet in his work . . . I could not bear that the poet in Shakespeare could never be seized and would never give an account of himself.' Undoubtedly this notion is partly behind Arnold's sonnet. Another note by the editor provides further illumination; this is an extract from a letter from Arnold to Arthur Hugh Clough:

* The sad news of whose too-early death comes as I correct the proofs of these pages.

Yet to *solve* the Universe as you try to do is as irritating as Tennyson's dawdling with its painted shell ... and yet I own that to *re-construct* the Universe is not a satisfactory attempt either—I keep saying, Shakespeare, Shakespeare, you are as obscure as life is.

The secrets of personal life, the riddle of existence—perhaps these *are* the things the general reader wants poetry to reveal. They aren't, however, in my experience, the things fellow practitioners would look to find answered in a poet's work, and if this is all Arnold is putting it would seem rather a writing-down on his part, a concession to popular feeling about poetry and about Shakespeare in particular.

Oddly enough, the further—indeed, the prime—obscurity I always found in that opening sentence arose from the real interest of poets in poetry, the verbal one. 'Others abide our question'— what the blazes does Arnold mean by 'abide'? One sees that it's a good word in the context: the long 'i' provides effective variety among the other vowel sounds of the line, and the 'd' sound enables 'our' to be pronounced without any awkward gap or pause for breath. But it isn't until one turns up the large Oxford Dictionary (which of course one might have done at a far earlier stage in one's uncertainty) and sees the seventeen meanings of the verb 'abide', that one realizes its built-in and ineradicable ambiguity. One might also, had one received an academic education, have considered the Victorian (indeed, possibly specifically Tennysonian) revival of the popularity of 'abide' from its King James's Bible days.

There are several kinds of gormlessness in the reading of poetry. I think the least venal is the ignorance and carelessness of youth. My appreciation of the marvellousness of Auden's *Poems* when I bought the book soon after its publication in 1930 was scarcely impaired by the misreadings of it in which I persisted for years.

Sir, no man's enemy, forgiving all
But will his negative inversion, be prodigal.

How long was it before I realized (or, more likely, someone told me) that 'will' was a noun not a verb, and that 'be prodigal' related not to the enemy but the 'Sir' to whom the sonnet was addressed? Undoubtedly our instinct for the good and the useful in contemporary poetry falls off with age, as does our minute interest in it. Probably the two declinations are connected. On the other hand, our general understanding of poetry increases, it seems to me. The poetic achievements of Walter de la Mare and D. H. Lawrence (to take two poets far from the first rank) I've quite recently come to admire through their skill and invention; a judgement, correct as it now appears, but one I was quite incapable of making in the ancient days when I over-valued Lawrence and discounted de la Mare. For it is the skilful parts of Lawrence and the inventive parts of de la Mare that matter, and not vice versa. Some of our increased understanding arises from our increased experience of life, but most of it, I guess, is arrived at by more patient reading, less obsession with the *zeitgeist*, and an absorption of critical precepts.

I want to say something about the last matter particularly. I have lived through a very great epoch of literary criticism. I read Eliot's criticism when I discovered his poetry in the late Twenties, and then went on to I. A. Richards. Leavis I've constantly gone back to. I read Empson's *Seven Types of Ambiguity* and *Some Versions of Pastoral* more or less as they came out. In the Fifties Donald Davie's criticism seemed even more valuable than the new sensible poetry which it accompanied. All these writers (and a few more names could be added to them) were part of the literary creativity of their time. They illuminated the tradition of that creativity and also, by teaching us how better to read poetic texts, enabled us to write better verse.

But I've lived, too, through a notable period of what I suppose one has to call academic criticism. This hesitation over nomenclature perhaps appears strange, speaking as I do in the University Examination Schools. Here, we are, if not ruled, certainly examined by academics. Some of you are fated to become academics yourselves. Indeed, all the 'creative' critics I've mentioned, except Eliot, are or were academics. At one time (and not so long ago) there was a sharp division between the academic and the creator. Some academics followed behind literary creativity at a distance that was more than respectful—positively laggardly. Moreover, the academic, trained in the technicalities of literature and of manuscripts and books, was readier to fulfil his function mainly among such technicalities. That situation has greatly altered and the reasons are plain. What was once thought of with admiration or scorn as the *avant garde* has been working in English literature for sixty years: in fact, all significant writing may be thought of as *avant garde*, though obviously some is more *avant* than the rest. Universities have grown so greatly that occupation in merely technical matters could hardly be found for their staffs and postgraduates. And (and perhaps this is the most telling) the example of the line of 'creative' critics has fired the academic to be creative also—to interpret beyond the text, to systematize his interpretation, to import other disciplines into his critical considerations.

So far as flexibility, open-mindedness and even mere extension of syllabuses into modern times are concerned, the change in the academic role might be conceived to be wholly admirable. But, alas, we know only too well that the 'creative academic', if I may term him so, has begun to interpose himself between the reader and the text—the text that, when all is said and done, is the reader's only proper study. It was, I'm sure, this sense of a vast literature to be ploughed through before the real literature is reached that prompted Auden to say once (in an article in the *Observer* called 'The Poet as Professor'), laying down a curriculum for what he called 'a Bardic College', that 'All critical writing, other than historical or textual, would be banned from the college library.'

'A vast literature', yes, and one, particularly in the United States, of variable helpfulness and sensibleness. It includes a good deal of inflated rubbish about the meaning of literary works and, worse perhaps, it has tended to create a limited and unreliable hierarchy of writers (especially modern writers) claiming a reader's attention today. But even the most distinguished part of it must be used, both by readers and teachers, with extreme discrimination. In this connection I commend a book called *Shakespeare and the Students* by

D. J. Enright, who is as wise and sparkling a critic as he is a poet. Enright says in his introduction (and the attitude is refreshingly manifest throughout the book's examination of four Shakespeare plays):

> In the first edition of *The Wheel of Fire*, that influential book on the interpretation of Shakespearean tragedy, G. Wilson Knight asserted that the persons, the characters of the plays, 'ultimately, are not human at all, but purely symbols of a poetic vision'. An unhappy consequence of this view of Shakespeare has been to make of his work an academic subject, remote from the merely 'human' concerns of the student. Many students have all too swiftly taken a further tip from L. C. Knights's reference to 'the necessary aloofness from a work of art', and art is then seen to be about what happened to *other* people—or better still, not to people at all, but just to symbols. Literature becomes something you are examined in at the end of the course, and you remain aloof from it at least until that grim day arrives with its inhuman concerns.
>
> M. C. Bradbrook once wrote, 'It is in the total situation rather than in the wrigglings of individual emotion that the tragedy lies.' One sees what she meant. But too often . . . this piece of advice has been construed as an excuse for not bothering with the uncomfortably complex wrigglings of Macbeth or Antony. The necessity of what we can still call 'modern' Shakespearean criticism cannot be denied. But there must be other teachers besides myself who feel that we have been rescued from the smoke and fire of romanticism only to be dropped into the hygenic incinerators of symbolism, imagery-computation, a curiously trite moralizing, and philosophizing of a sort so primitive as undoubtedly to have contributed to the discredit which literature has fallen into among the serious-minded.

But, as I've perhaps needlessly said, there have been great and true academic critics in my lifetime and, of course, in this very field of Shakespearean studies. The work of Dr Alice Walker comes at once to mind. Her book *Textual Problems of the First Folio* not only irradiates Shakespeare's plays: its methods and terminology, its account of the fate of a poet's words after they have left his desk, also reverberate in the imagination. The book lies behind a short poem of mine called 'Versions of Love' and I would hope any reader of that would also have read Dr Walker. I for one have no objection to critical nit-picking, provided it's of the technical sort, and allied with brain-power. What a relief, particularly after some recent studies and lives of Shakespeare, both fictional and allegedly factual, to return to the daddy of them all, E. K. Chambers's two volumes of 1930, *William Shakespeare: A Study of Facts and Problems*. Perhaps because everything can be found in his pages (right down to the painted wall of the Tudor room in the Cornmarket) masterfully displayed, that Chambers can be so brilliantly commonsensical. Discussing the chronology of the plays, for instance, he quite casually throws out the following remarks:

> In reading Shakespeare, I feel that there is a great deal of level stress, and that in many lines there are very few strong stresses. These features may vary at different periods, but the subject still wants working out. How far the actors emphasized stress, where it was optional we cannot say. Polonius commended the 'good accent' of a highly stressed speech; but he was no judge.

Here, it seems to me, we have some valuable hints on a matter which has bedevilled Shakespearean productions ever since I went, as a boy, to see those of Sir Frank Benson and less-celebrated touring actor-managers. The measured, inclined to be hammy style of speech that Benson presumably inherited from the Victorian Shakespeareans, quickly gave way, in my early days, to a gabble that became quite a convention. The gabble may be regarded as an appropriate counterpart of the quite healthy revolution in production, that by dispensing with intervals and elaborate sets enabled a rapid succession of scenes to be staged and consequently more of Shakespeare's text to be actually played. Since in the gabble a good deal of meaning was lost — a meaning that because of the changes in vocabulary and syntax, and modern incomprehension of external reference the brisk modern producer

would in any case have regarded as irrecoverable audience-wise
— gimmicks were introduced to restore the consequent falling off
of interest. Wax comically elongated actors' noses, elderly
characters were frantically palsied: the plays were set in Victorian
England or the Austro-Hungarian Empire; and played in Regency
muslin or modern dinner-jackets. In more recent times we have
seen, in some productions, the reflection of the symbolic view of
Shakespearean characterization referred to by Enright, where the
action takes place in some formalized never-never land.

The question of how the verse should be spoken remains. I fear
that the old tradition of ham has never really been sliced off. In the
parody of Shakespearean productions, stemming from the comic
genius of Jonathan Miller in the *Beyond the Fringe* revue at the end
of the Fifties, the satire was directed mainly against conventionalized action — mutual forearm claspings, back-clappings,
and the like — but it also paid attention to both the gabbled and
hammy styles of poetry-speaking. In general actors can't speak
verse. The irritating singing diction, taught by the academies
(presumably so as to avoid monotony of pitch), persists even in
actors who escaped early or never attended the academies. The
problem of keeping the rhythm but reading for sense seems, too,
to be beyond them. Indeed, the business isn't easy to bring off. In
general, a much slower, more thoughtful and less emotional
delivery is to be recommended, with the easier effects of pathos
and comedy strictly avoided.

(One might interpolate here a point made by Francis Berry in
his suggestive book *Poetry and the Physical Voice*, that only in his
non-dramatic work, conspicuously in the sonnets, did Shakespeare
seemingly compose for his own voice. In the plays he used the
familiar voices of his fellow actors as 'surrogates, or instruments'.
Mr Berry's lengthy discussion of the matter should be read: I
would here merely add a rather different and simpler observation
— that because of their complexity the sonnets would on the whole
require a slow reading, with the emphasis on the words vital for
sense rather than on the stresses of the verse, and that this might
well be done by the poet himself, who quite soon would have

forgotten, a common experience of poets, what meaning he had intended. Such required rediscovery of meaning is also implicit in a good deal of the verse of the dramas. This view chimes with Chambers's remark about level stress.)

So, too, though one wouldn't want at all to go back to anything like Irving's mahogany furniture and live horses, a setting is required for the plays that doesn't positively impose non-realism. Much can be taken in the theatre by way of convention but, as A. C. Bradley realized, Shakespeare's plays (despite the symbols, the verse, the words, the staggering intellectual genius) are finally about human affairs and need a human setting. In his introduction to the Arden edition of Shakespeare's poems, F. T. Prince has a penetrating passage:

> In the language, the poetry, the poet lives one life, and in his vision of the subject he lives another. He creates the poem in a kind of double consciousness, in two concurrent lives, made possible by intense activity of mind and feeling. We who read can share this double consciousness; indeed such a detached yet intense participation in the imagined lives of beings other than ourselves is the end of all art. Try to explain it, and you initiate an explanation of human consciousness itself, with all that may be entailed.

Professor Prince was writing about Shakespeare's two narrative poems, but his words will remind us, if we need reminding, of the significance to Shakespeare and to ourselves of the characters in the plays. In the history of our literature since Shakespeare the poet's 'double consciousness' has been weakened in the moiety that offers to interest us 'in the imagined lives of beings other than ourselves', for that role has largely been taken over by novelists and prose dramatists. In lyrical poetry, the growingly dominant mode since the Romantic Revolution, the only fully imagined life is often that of the poet himself — with all the dangers of narrowness, self-indulgence and indeed sheer boredom that entails. But yes, in Shakespeare, as in Jane Austen and George Eliot and Dickens, we give ourselves wholly to this mysterious

6

human trait of yielding up our intellectual and emotional concern to a set of people who never were, not necessarily in an un-sophicated way but certainly without reservations as to the convention, or degree of importance compared with 'real' life, that the business involves. And when we see the plays on the stage (where they were meant for) a further process takes place, also mysterious, and of a fundamental simplicity, even crudity, which nevertheless ought to enhance (and does enhance, if the ingredients are right) the effect the poet aimed for. In the theatre the creatures of the poet's imagination are given living human form. So that we are offered to be turned up (or turned on) not merely by the fictional King Lear but by the fictional King Lear in the person, say, of Sir Donald Wolfit, with all Wolfit's traits as actor and as man, traits that will by no means meet with our uniform approval.

The process doesn't stop short before Shakespeare's late romances, sometimes thought to be supremely non-naturalistic. Prospero is often considered a dry, even wearisome figure; the magician's omnipotence not made much less inhuman by flashes of puritanism and testiness. The best Prospero I have ever seen was played by Michael Hordern, without the aid of white whiskers: a man of middle-age, experience not precluding further experience, fully-conscious humour not avoiding unwilled comic aspects of the persona — a reading quite within the text. Above all, Mr Hordern gave up as little as possible to tradition and conven-tion the naturalism learnt in acting in plays of our time. Of course, naturalism is itself a kind of convention — or at least it stems from rapidly changing manners. But as one always wonders why opera is still acted in a style that seems to us utterly unnaturalistic, so one must be impatient with Shakespearean productions that are not contemporary in that sense, even more now that cinema and television drama have accustomed us to what our grandfathers would have regarded as baffling under-playing. I think there has yet to be, even on the Box, a Shakespeare play presented as close to life as it is visibly and orally lived, as say, even *Softly Softly* — though what might be done in this area was more than indicated by James Mactaggart's direction of *The Duchess of Malfi* on BBC2 on 10 October, 1972.

We lyric poets have filched much from Shakespeare's enormous cast. We have used him as a shorthand for worlds we failed to create ourselves. Apropos of *The Tempest*, it can be seen how superior is Auden's *The Sea and the Mirror*, which uses the people of that play, to another long poem of his middle period, *The Age of Anxiety*, where the protagonists are of Auden's own invention — superior, I mean, simply in the amount of depth of life we feel the characters possess. Some years ago I read in another Arden introduction, Frank Kermode's to this same play of *The Tempest*, of Shakespeare's preoccupation in 'these last plays with the theme of reconciliation, and the survival into a new world of the children of those who had quarrelled'. I was taken by the phrase (which meatily summarizes the modern view of the plays) because being of an age myself to have seen a new generation grow to maturity I had been thinking of the subject as one for literary work. But it never for a moment struck me that the business could be brought off in a poem, and even had I been a dramatist I should have written in prose. My Leontes-Prospero figure had to be placed in a solid naturalistic setting (he is the hero of my novel *My Child, My Sister*). Though poetry in our time has succeeded in recovering the language and situations of ordinary life, it isn't capable, as literature has developed, of emulating the psychological interplay of the characters of the novel. Even where the poet assumes a mask not his own, poetry is now essentially a monologue, and possibly there is a danger (maybe this is meant when the 'death' of the novel is referred to) that the novel may become a monologue, too.

One of the plates in the great work of Shakespearean research and criticism by Sir Edmund Chambers already referred to is of the bust in the monument in Stratford Church. Familiar though it is, one always gets a slight shock seeing this effigy, whether in reproduction or actuality. Perhaps this is partly due to one's even greater familiarity with reproductions of the Droeshout engraving, part of the title page to the First Folio — the image there being altogether more intellectual and refined. The Stratford monument Shakespeare is a stoutish man, the moustache curled upwards in the style of a pilot of the Second War. The eyes are prominent and outward-looking, the mouth slightly open: features of a keen observer of the exterior world (and incidentally those of one slightly apoplectic — we recall the legend of Shakespeare's death following a boozing session with Drayton and Jonson). Though the image may, as I say, surprise the romantic view of the Bard, I find it entirely convincing. As Aldous Huxley once remarked in a letter: 'Fertile inventors and narrators and genre painters have all been rather burly, genial fellows.' So, too, we may feel, must have been one who was able to abstract for poetry so much of life as it is lived.

One can't really regret the division of literary art into the two great rivers of poetry and fiction: each has its marvels, many arising from the very business of specialization. But when we consider the work of a modern poet to whom we can unquestionably, I think, affix the label 'great' — Wallace Stevens, and his case is not untypical — I believe that for all its bulk, skill and invention it encloses a serious lack, the lack of a detailed realism and the unfulfilment of our interest, in Professor Prince's words, 'in the imagined lives of other beings'. No doubt those two things must usually go together. Stevens himself may well have been conscious of an obligation not carried out: he is constantly, even in short poems, producing characters, but they are usually mere fantastic sketches. Certainly in his critical prose, in his letters (and in his poems also), he is obsessed with the relation between literature and reality. Towards the end of his life he wrote a poem that despite its brevity and comparative simplicity summed up with intense feeling his long years of poetic work. Like so many of us, it is upon Shakespeare that he calls for image and sanction. 'Ariel', he begins:

Ariel was glad he had written his poems.

The last two stanzas, speaking of his poetry, provide the title of the poem:

It was not important that they should survive.
What mattered was that they should bear
Some lineament or character,

Some affluence, if only half-perceived,
In the poverty of their words,
Of the planet of which they were part.

He called the poem 'The Planet on the Table', perhaps with a
thought for the volume of collected Shakespeare as well as of
collected Stevens, but in the modest hesitations of the poem's
words we see Stevens's genuine reservations about his own work —
possibly the consciousness that Shakespeare's work is not only a
planet on the table but also a planet in the theatre among masses
and many sorts of humanity.

It will have been seen that I've been merely sniffing cautiously
round the circumference of the Bard. It seemed rather bad that
during five years I've scarcely, so far as I recall, even uttered the
name of Shakespeare. I've always wanted to add my half page to the
great heap of Shakespearean criticism but have long realized that I
lacked the intellect and insight to do anything of the 'creative' sort.
From the academic sort my education (or, rather, absence of it)
and previous occupation debarred me. (I've even been forestalled
in possibly writing about Shakespeare in his conjectured years as
lawyer's clerk: as to that I can only add that his forensic imagery,
commendably accurate though it is, is unlikely to have come from
one actually engaged in the law, for the closer one is to the
technicalities of an occupation the less likely one is to use them in
one's creative non-occupation.) Though once I did think I'd made
a small discovery. In the opening scene of *The Merchant of Venice*
where Antonio and his two fellow Venetian Rotarians are
discussing the import and export business, Salario says how
worried *he* would be if he had ships and merchandise at sea:

I should not see the sandy hour-glass run
But I should think of shallows and of flats,
And see my wealthy Andrew dock'd in sand.

The word 'Andrew' is in italics in the Quarto and Dr Johnson's suggestion that it was the name of a ship has been generally accepted. But (so the story continues) no contemporary ship of that name could be found until, in a letter to *The Times Literary Supplement* dated 27 December 1928, Professor Kuhl advanced the proposition that Shakespeare was referring to the Spanish ship, the *St Andrew*, captured during the Cadiz expedition of 1596 and brought to England. Kuhl's proposition received critical assent and now appears in all the notes. The point is of some importance because of the dating of the play: the news of the Cadiz expedition didn't reach the Court until 30 July 1596, and this date now forms the earliest limit for composition, the latest being 22 July 1598, the date of entry of the play in the Stationers' Register.

The uneasiness about all this felt by anyone who has been in the Royal Navy is that 'the Andrew' is common naval slang for the Royal Navy itself. Surely there must be some connection between this and the name so casually tossed out by Salario. Could the *St Andrew* have been so celebrated both that Shakespeare's reference would have been generally understood and that it should have given its name to the whole service? Unlikely. The New English Dictionary provided no help. A useful volume called *The Seaman's Manual*, issued to me as part of my kit when I was called up into the Navy in 1941, said that prior to the accession of James I Scottish ships sailed under the cross of St Andrew. Though in my experience the Scots form a substantial proportion of the Navy's lower deck and are a masterful race, it seemed improbable that they had imposed their nomenclature (if indeed it was used in that way) on the combined fleets after 1603. To cut a tedious story short, I found after consulting a number of slang dictionaries (which by no means agreed) that the term 'the Andrew' seems to date only from the mid-nineteenth century. It may be rhyming slang — man of war, Andrew Millar; Millar being said to be an early contractor of fresh provisions for the Navy. Others say that the derivation is from Andrew Walker, a notorious press gang tough. Finally, a book by John S. Farmer called *Slang and its Analogues* dealt the death-blow to my academicism. The author's entry under 'Andrew Millar, sub. (nautical)' ran as follows:

A curious cant name for a ship of war; sometimes simply ANDREW. Its origin is quite unknown; but it has been pointed out that Antonio (sic), in the *Merchant of Venice*, speaks of one of his vessels as his 'wealthy Andrew'; and it has been conjectured that in this case the ship was named after the celebrated Admiral Andrea Doria, who died in 1560. But to trace any connection between this Andrew, however general the use of the name may have become, and the Andrew Millar of modern sailors' slang, would be difficult.

Curious that this book was published nearly forty years before Professor Kuhl's epoch-making letter to *The Times Literary Supplement*!

It may seem nit-picking indeed to be trying to assign a play to one of a trio of years. But Shakespeare developed so rapidly during these years (during every year) that the matter has curiosity value at least. Besides, apart from the Andrew business, there are some (fairly inconclusive) indications putting the earliest limiting date as far back as 1594. *The Merchant of Venice* has long struck me as one of the very few plays of Shakespeare that, as the phrase goes, one wouldn't cross the road to see. This, at first blush, would incline one to put it with *King John*, so to speak, rather than with *Much Ado About Nothing*. But trying to pin down one's feelings about the play, one sees that there's nothing inherently boring in it. Perhaps the main trouble is the tradition of playing Shylock as a stage Jew and presenting the worthless *jeunesse dorée* of the play as wholly virtuous. A recent TV production unconsciously revealed the shallowness and self-regard of Bassanio and Co, while following the tradition. The camera's prying eye was a true critic, and perhaps some deficiencies of playing rammed the point home. One's sense is that Shakespeare had ambivalent emotions about his materials, and one would like to see a production which brought out the ambiguity by depicting Shylock as a figure not in the least outré (and, after all, we must feel that Shakespeare's view of the

Jew, like our own liberal view of the black, though taking into account common prejudice, seeks always for the common factors between the two religions, the two races), and the young opposition for what it was, a set of rather feeble idlers dependent on Antonio's and Portia's hard cash. Not that anything morally, or even aesthetically, plain could come out of the play, any more than it can come out of *Much Ado* (one thinks of 'Kill Claudio'). So one's inclination is to put it as late as possible — even giving time for the name of the ship to pass into popular usage! 1597 was a year in which the scholars don't seem to have found much going on in Shakespeare's workshop. It was the year of the purchase of New Place: the possible commuting between London and Stratford could be reflected in the Venice and Belmont scenes. The year also saw some Shakespearean litigation. 1596 was a bad year for weather: 1597 must have been better and the Belmont night is particularly salubrious. Into such dubious realms is one quickly led when attempting Shakespearean criticism! However, to pick the final nit, Kuhl in his *TLS* letter thought that the passage in question couldn't have been written before the autumn of 1597 because he believed it referred to the disastrous expedition to the Azores in that year, when the *St Andrew* was one of the ships scattered in the storm. The introduction to the Arden edition argues, with some show of evidence, for the previous year, but in any case poets aren't always as topical as journalists.

Such is the bulk of writing about Shakespeare that even the most modest aperçu is likely to have been anticipated. After preparing the foregoing passage about *The Merchant of Venice*, I found that W. H. Auden (in *The Dyer's Hand*) has classed the work 'among Shakespeare's "Unpleasant Plays"', using the Shavian category. His point is that the 'fairy-world of Belmont is incompatible with the historical reality of money-making Venice', and so the claim to virtuousness of Belmont and our natural attraction to it, are called into question. One might add, apropos of this reminder of Shakespeare's dramatic delineation of mercantile capitalism, that the play (together perhaps with the city scenes of the plays that followed, the two parts of *Henry IV*) was the start of a road not taken by the playwright — a more or less realistic depiction of the new bourgeois society. That development was, of course, followed by some other dramatists of the period. Its mainly comic implications would very soon have ceased to be attractive to Shakespeare: besides, the political and philosophical problems involved would have been very arduous to solve in dramatic and poetical form. Like so many great writers (Tolstoy, Dickens and George Eliot come to mind) Shakespeare is inclined to set his work backward in time, avoiding issues that may prove merely topical or ephemeral. And he often makes, as do Milton and Yeats, a virtue of a world-view already eroded by intellectual speculation and economic development: the strategy, or constitutional cast of mind, certainly leads to the creation of tragedy.

Others abide our question. Thou art free.
We ask and ask — Thou smilest and art still,
Out-topping knowledge. For the loftiest hill,
Who to the stars uncrowns his majesty,

Planting his steadfast footsteps in the sea,
Making the heaven of heavens his dwelling-place,
Spares but the cloudy border of his base
To the foiled searching of mortality.

Dr Leavis, in *Education and the University*, thought Arnold's comparison of Shakespeare to 'the loftiest hill' quite inappropriate:

Had Arnold realized in the least what purports to be his theme, Shakespeare's greatness or inscrutability, a mountain could never have presented itself to him as a symbol for it. There is nothing remote or austerely or inhumanly exalted about Shakespeare, whose genius is awe-inspiring by the inwardness and completeness of its humanity.

Well said, we may think. Shakespeare is a difficult poet, but then all good English poets have been difficult (with a few exceptions!). The language is in favour of difficulty — we remember those seventeen instances of 'abide' and such things as the comparatively

limited but challenging opportunity for rhyme in English. But
Leavis is right to remind us that Shakespeare is no mandarin, set
apart, like Paul Valéry, say, by the force of his intellect and the
specialization of his interests. Caroline Spurgeon told us long ago,
in her book *Shakespeare's Imagery*, that 'The great bulk of
Shakespeare's metaphors and similes are drawn from the simplest
everyday things seen and observed'. We are so often conscious,
even when the persons are exalted and the affairs violent, that the
plays come out of the experience of private life, an experience we
all share. Even in the sparse biographical details that have come
down to us we sense the psychological yeast set working awe-
somely by events — Shakespeare's two elder sisters, both dead in
childhood before the poet himself was born; the arrival of his
younger siblings; his pre-marital sexual experience as a mere
youth; the birth to him of boy and girl twins and the death of the
boy as a child; the death of his father; the arrival of a grand-
daughter. So, too, we have a hint or two of the strange coincidences
and repetitions (paralleling the puns and connections of the subconscious) that appear in every life — that his mother's maiden
name was Arden; that his dead son proved to be named after the
Prince of Denmark. In other words, we know enough of
Shakespeare to receive from his work a sense of the common
human behind it. At least we can assent to the end of Matthew
Arnold's sonnet:

> *All pains the immortal spirit must endure,*
> *All weakness which impairs, all griefs which bow,*
> *Find their sole speech in that victorious brow.*

— Though taking Leavis's adverse comments on the poem a little
farther, we may just boggle at that 'sole', for other poets have quite
decently rendered the pains, weaknesses and griefs referred to. In
the need of the metre for a monosyllabic epithet, Arnold seems to
have been seduced by alliteration into something illogical and
inappropriate, as earlier on he put in 'footsteps' after 'steadfast', a
ludicrous trope, Leavis points out, for a hill.

At the university we may learn what earlier is often obscured — that literature is a continuous, never-ending creative human process. Its neat epochs and grand monuments are made by the critics not the creators. Its works are as open to us to challenge and enjoy as anything written today. Perhaps it's slightly unfortunate that evaluation and enjoyment have to be tested within these walls. But that need not destroy the sense on the one hand of literature's abiding vitality and on the other of its creators being more or less ordinary specimens of humanity, with all humanity's frailties as well as its potential.

I think it was Enid Starkie, of still lively memory, who first conceived the notion that the occupant of the Oxford Chair of Poetry should be a practising poet, and masterfully carried the idea into practical effect. The drawbacks are obvious, frequently embarrassingly so, but at least the warts of a creator are in the Schools and at university and college societies presented to view. And perhaps the lesson is conveyed that going down eventually from here, from a life of emotional experience set among books and many other trophies of culture, into a world and an ageing on the whole inimical to such things, need not mean an utter abandonment of the striving for standards, and for the better understanding of the old and the new in literature, our notable and idiosyncratic poetry in particular.

Index